PILGRIMAGE TO THE REBIRTH

Erlo van Waveren

Erlo van Waveren

Pilgrimage to the Rebirth

DAIMON

Part One of this book was originally published by Samuel Weiser, Inc., New York, in 1978.

ISBN 3-85630-570-X (hard cover)
ISBN 3-85630-571-8 (paperback)

PRINTED IN CANADA

This tale of my spirit is dedicated
to my much loved and lovely wife
Ann.

Her courage and unfailing search for truth,
her support of the timeless memories of
my spirit, and her sweet curiosity gave
my Self the opportunity to write this tale
of my psychic life.

On this page, Ann and I want to pay tribute to Carl Gustav Jung. It is Dr. Jung – the august Carl – who has given us the tools to understand more of our psyche, of which we are, to quote him, "so pitifully unaware." We love that man very much, and he often symbolizes for us the great Wise Man in our dreams.

Contents

A Biographical Note

Before anything else came the Unconscious: Erlo van Waveren, at his great cost, first discovered that he could not ignore it; then he found himself directed, indeed sometimes almost monopolized by it, so that, in the end, it mattered most to him. These two parts of *Pilgrimage to the Rebirth* are the result. And they are worth reading, not only because the Unconscious always has something to teach us, but also because Erlo van Waveren was transformed by his contact with Carl Gustav Jung. What was quickened in him matters to us: it is both a commentary and a continuation of Jung's own reflections on humankind and the psyche at the beginning of the Aquarian Age.

That Erlo van Waveren should one day be interested in Jung, or in psychology, or in the psyche, would, in his youth, have seemed highly unlikely. The youngest of a large, upper-class Dutch family, he was expected by his formidable and single-minded father to do what his older brothers had done: go into the family business. The van Waverens owned and ran a large bulb and seed business. There were many employees to direct, many fields, in Holland, in Germany and elsewhere to be managed. Salesmen were needed as well as agronomists and businessmen: more than enough occupations to keep Erlo and his brothers busy.

There was also a large, and on the whole close, family: cousins, aunts, great-aunts – not to mention Erlo's three sisters, all tied not just by affection or shared position, but also by very deep roots. Beyond the grandparents and great-grandparents, the van Waverens could trace their ancestors to the early seventeenth century. They were quintessentially Dutch, anciently established people who belonged where they were and owned a good deal of what they saw around them. Still, the end of the nineteenth century was also a time for renewal, for economic growth. Erlo's father, a stout man with an often belligerent expression, typically built a large, new, and inordinately ugly house. There was room for the seven children and the servants. Hours were fixed, the household well regulated; and Erlo's mother's first duty was to make sure all was in order.

*

Erlo was born in 1902, at a time when the certainties of bourgeois life seemed rock-solid and eternal. Worse, perhaps, were a certain narrowness of mind, and the typically Dutch smugness, which in turn entailed a sense of being, deservedly, among the elect. The van Waverens were not a religious household; but Erlo's father still had a very Calvinist sense of predestination. He was one of the chosen ones, if not before God, then certainly before his fellow-businessmen and many relatives.

As for Erlo, his future seemed obviously set. Like his brothers, he was mostly educated at home; the other children he saw – there were not many of them – were those of families like his own. When he grew up, he would join the family business, marry the right sort of girl and father the kind of children who would, in their turn, do the same. It was a rigid, unchanging world, and one which had little regard for anything beyond the most conventional activities.

At least, Erlo's mother, devoted wife though she was, understood that other things could matter: books, music, art all had a place in her world, and she passed those tastes on to her younger son. Still, it was his father who made the decisions; and so, as soon as Erlo had finished his schooling, he went to work for the firm. In short order, he was sent, as a salesman, to the United States; and that was when his unconscious began to make its presence felt.

In those last years at home, Erlo had not been happy – but he did not quite know why. Nor did it ever occur to him that there was anything he could do about it – it was simply a question of hoping things would get better; but coming to America taught him something: in this new country, he found an openness of mind and spirit, a tolerance, even an eagerness for change; and it was all immensely appealing. Already in Europe, he had begun meeting people who were not part of his family's circle, people who were interested in philosophy and psychology, whose interests were the very opposite of the dry certainties his father embodied. In America, there were more such people, and it was easier to meet them. Suddenly, Holland seemed very small, very hidebound, altogether too limited and too limiting.

Still, he was unhappy – in part because he hated his job as sales representative for the family firm, in part because he felt a deep lack in his personal life. Even falling in love failed to cure that: he was happier for a while, but not contented; and when the romance fell apart, he was more than ever the prey of his growing doubts, of his increasing feelings of misery. As he knew too well, he remained, after all, a young man defined by his family's business and rules. It was a while before he could gather enough courage to leave the first and change the last; but, in the end, he had no choice.

There followed a period of apparent hopelessness. In his late twenties, no longer the son his father expected, not yet his own man, Erlo found himself without a career, indeed without a job; all he knew was that he could not lead the settled life which had been planned for him. What was he to do? Where and how was he to live? Who, in fact, was he? These were questions he could not answer, and for a while, he saw himself as a man without a purpose.

In this darkness, however, there was one light: aware that the misery came from within himself, he understood that he needed to know himself better. Although, at the beginning of the Thirties, psychoanalysis was neither as accepted nor as easily entered as it is today, he found an analyst. And that was when, slowly and painfully, he began to get glimpses of who he was and what he was about.

The analyst in question, Ann Moyer, was a Jungian. In the mid-Twenties, working in New York for Dr. Samuel Seabury, she had been trained as a psychologist. But although Dr. Seabury was well-known, and seemed then at the forefront of the field, Miss Moyer felt that he lacked depth. Something, she felt, was being left out; and that was when she cabled Jung to ask whether she might work with him. To her surprise, Jung told her to come; and she was trained, partly by him directly, partly by disciples such as Toni Wolff. When, some years later, she moved back to New York, it was as a Jungian analyst.

It is one of the distinguishing characteristics of Jungian psychology that it does not limit itself to the individual components of the psyche. Myths (which reflect fears and hopes common to all humankind), shared history, and a spiritual dimension are also recognized as key parts of all of us. Of course, there is a personal goal: individuation, the full realization and integration of each individual psyche is the ultimate object of every person willing to work with the psyche. And it can be reached, sometimes partly through analysis, occasionally without it, through an increasing knowledge of one's own unconscious which, in turn, allows the recognition of the neuroses which are holding us back and the strengths which can propel us to the next stage of development.

A good Jungian analyst will therefore try, not only to make life more bearable for the client, but also to increase self-knowledge while providing the tools which can be used, eventually, without outside help. Dreams, fantasies, creative imagination are among them, and it is the analyst's task to make people better able to communicate with their own psyche. Eventually, these tools should become so familiar that the analyst's intercession is no longer needed. For, indeed, communication with one's psyche should not be a brief exercise resorted to only in a crisis, but a lifetime's undertaking.

Naturally, Miss Moyer knew all this. She was also aware that the psyche has vast dimensions and that she was a new analyst. At first, all went well; then, after some months, Erlo began having dreams of such scope that she no longer felt able to interpret them: the material was simply too complex and too potent. There was only one thing to do: she told her client that he needed to see Jung; and so he, in turn, went to Zürich.

*

As it turned out, Jung agreed that Erlo's dreams were "big" dreams in that they connected to key myths; thus they had a more than individual meaning. Of course, there were also personal issues. It became clear, in the course of the analysis, who Erlo was: a man with a powerful unconscious whose guidance must be followed, whose demands must be met. There was more: intuition, for instance, and empathy, two of the key qualities any good analyst must have; and soon his dreams showed specifically what he was to do: become an analyst. There was no doubt, Jung told him, that was his job; and so, for the next fifty years it turned out to be.

As to the life he was to lead, that, too, soon became obvious. Upon returning to New York, Erlo resumed contact with Ann Moyer, not as a patient, but, first as a friend, and then as a suitor. Miss Moyer, in her early forties and still unmarried, also felt sure that she had at last found the man with whom she could spend the rest of her life. There was, however, a serious problem: an analyst should not be emotionally involved with her patient, much less marry him. Still, the therapist-client relationship had ended when Erlo went off to Zürich. Now, the two of them decided, there was only one thing to do. They were in Zürich for the summer anyway, so they consulted Jung; and with his approval and encouragement, they were married.

Had that not happened, these two books would certainly not have been written. Ann and Erlo's marriage was conventionally happy by any definition: husband and wife were in love with each other until the time they died. They shared tastes, interests, occupations. They had the same profession, they liked the same friends. Except for the war years, when it was no longer possible to cross the Atlantic, both felt renewed by their annual summer stays in Zürich. There they saw Jung, until his death in 1961, and their other friends in the Jungian community. There, beginning in the sixties, Erlo was free to spend time on what, more and more, came to be his most crucial work.

This is where the extra dimension of Ann and Erlo's marriage comes in. As analysts, they had always paid particular attention to their unconscious, and it was soon clear to both of them that Erlo had the capacity to be a mystic. Ann, on the other hand, was more down-to-earth, more firmly grounded, and very able to spot vagueness or exaggeration. She also had the strength to support Erlo when the demands of his unconscious seemed unreasonable or painful – while he, at the same time, gave her the lift, the broader horizons she needed. Neither could have functioned half as well without the other. Each was thoroughly aware of it, and recognized in the other the qualities missing in him or herself.

Thus, when Erlo began to have the dreams on which *Pilgrimage to the Rebirth* is based, it was Ann who gave him the strength to work them through, who asked the tough questions and who confirmed that this was a real message, not some ungrounded fantasy. These were not easy dreams. Their central figures proved to be what Jung called "ancestral figures," but Erlo, unwillingly at first, came to see them as earlier incarnations.

Whether an analyst should interpret his dreams as describing earlier lives was, obviously, an important question. The world, after all, counts many people who posit earlier incarnations (usually as a highly dramatic figure) because they need to compensate for their current frustrations. His first reaction, therefore, was to take these figures as symbols; but that was precisely what his following dreams would not allow him to do.

Here, once again, Ann was of the greatest help. Highly intelligent and precise, she was not about to be swept away by vague, unrealistic, romantic notions; but dreams cannot be ignored. And to her, as well, it seemed increasingly certain that Erlo was dealing with earlier lives. The pain that accompanied these steps was itself a sort of confirmation: Erlo dreaded the appearance of these figures, struggled against accepting them for what they claimed to be. In fact, he earnestly wished to be rid of the whole process.

That next summer, he went to Jung, told him what he had been experiencing, and asked him whether it was simply the symptom of a neurosis. Jung assured him that it was no such thing and asked Erlo whether he had sought these revelations, exclaiming in relief when Erlo assured him he had not, "Well, then, you'll be all right." For, in fact, the process was not without danger: twice it brought about serious physical illnesses.

Even more important than the assurance Jung had given, that these figures were indeed to be considered as incarnations, was the certainty Jung expressed to Erlo about reincarnation, and about having himself been through a number of lives. These conversations were highly confidential at the time, and in Jung's lifetime, Erlo repeated them to no one except Ann. Still, they provided a further legitimacy to the work he had undertaken: there was much to be learned from these incarnations, about the past, but also about the coming transformations.

Every two thousand years or so, it seems, as we pass from one sign of the Zodiac to the next, the Zeitgeist, the collective psyche, undergoes a transformation. Together with it comes a feeling of being lost, a sense of spiritual drift, a breakdown of accepted mores. That is just what we are seeing now; and the importance of the dream material Erlo experienced over nearly forty years is that it provides some understanding, some guidance, even, to help us deal with these changes. In method, in spirit, everything Erlo did was thoroughly Jungian; but in content (for this area, at least), his message begins where Jung stopped. Here is a story about the passing of one age and the coming of another. It begins in *Pilgrimage to the Rebirth*, Volume I, which was published in Erlo's lifetime. He did not live to finish the second part of *Pilgrimage to the Rebirth*. Theodore Young, in his preface explains how the book was brought to publishable form. Certainly, its contents were too important to be left, dormant, in manuscript form. They are the result of Erlo's lifework. He wanted them to be made available. He would have hoped that they might provide a little light through our present darkness.

Olivier Bernier

Preface

With the advent of the new aeon, the Age of Aquarius, the problem of uniting the opposites within the psyche will be a major concern of civilization if it is to survive the next two thousand years. Evil, already on the rise, will come to the fore, and mankind will have to deal with it psychologically, not sweep it under the rug and dismiss it as just a privation of good, this having been the case for most of the last two thousand years. As C.G. Jung says in *Aion*, "This problem can be solved neither by philosophy, nor by economics, nor by politics, but only by the individual human being, via his experience of the living spirit...."[1]

The second part of *Pilgrimage to the Rebirth* continues the journey of Erlo van Waveren's soul, a journey in quest of the Self. It begins after the magical birth of Aquarius, an inner God-image who is a more complete symbol of the Self than the one-sided figure of Christ. The text touchingly records Aquarius' development and what is required of him and of humanity to meet the challenge of his reign. Since the book is in the form of a myth, it is not only an example of the process of individuation for a single human being – the author – but it is also a glimpse of the evolution of human consciousness in the course of the aeon to come.

During the Aquarian Age, humanity will be forced to come to terms with itself, to endure its own darkness, as uncharted roads, unknown vistas and suppressed worlds are brought into the light of day. In the text before us, Aquarius, made human in these pages, redeems Lucifer, the Light of Darkness, in a terrible night fight of changing aeons, thereby answering

[1] C.W. 9, 11, par. 142, 1959.

Christ's prayers for wholeness and uniting him with his shadow in the psychic manifestation of the Godhead. Thus, in the soul of Erlo van Waveren, and in all humanity, man, an image was born of the archetype of the Self that possesses, for the first time, the capacity to reconcile all of creation – the Dark as well as the Light, Death as well as Life, the Feminine as well as the Masculine, the Body as well as the Spirit, Earth as well as Heaven. The divine energies are flowing equally into opposing parts of the psyche, and the power of the Godhead to bring the contrasting forces together is being put into human hands. (We can see that happening all around us, now, as we approach the new millennium.)

But, as the text points out, with that widening power an individual consciousness will now be required to abide the rising tide of blackness waiting for redemption. We will no longer be able to live unconsciously like a fish; Aquarius, as Redeemer and Savior, will demand a level of awareness that will represent the next advance in the history of human consciousness. Whether we progress to that stage depends upon our willingness to sacrifice the ego and be redeemer and savior to ourselves. For only then, as Erlo van Waveren tells us stunningly, will we experience the holiness of our individual being, will we experience the power of the archetype to unite the inborn duality of life. And when we do, we not only expand our own consciousness, but add to the consciousness of the Godhead as well.

Thus, a devoted effort to turn inward, to undergo the psychological experience of death and rebirth, will be the main task of the Aquarian Age, and individuation the way of fulfilling it.

*

The record of a myth lived out is always the most difficult kind of writing. One is hooked by the unconscious to participate in a universal drama; to seek out the nature of one's soul in the hope that what you have done will expand your vision of the world and help others who are seeking to find their own answers. You identify with the material coming up, and it is a painstaking effort to keep your sanity. Many times the author sought to withdraw from his commitment to the unconscious, to abandon the journey to the root of his being. It seemed too difficult at times, too destructive to the ego to continue. But, as the author notes, he was compelled to go on; Aquarius was always around the corner to pull him back into himself.

Erlo van Waveren's chronicle of a soul's journey was assembled from his dream books, diaries and the notes that accumulated over many years. A working draft of the entire manuscript, parts I and II, was completed in the late 1960's, and in 1978, after much rewriting and editing, the first half of *Pilgrimage to the Rebirth* was published. Editing of the second half was scheduled to begin in the fall of '85, after the author's completion, in longhand, of a third manuscript, but his untimely death made that impossible. Several years later, editing did begin, under the auspices of the Foundation which bears his name. It was an arduous task, since without the author's presence, his full intentions could not be expressed. His absence may be evident at times, inasmuch as the text is obscure in parts. Had the author been alive, it would also have been more detailed. Nevertheless, that lack of labor in no way subtracts from the meaningfulness of the manuscript. His integrity and conviction, his Biblical spirit and inspirational thoughts are what illumines his writing and will be remembered.

Erlo van Waveren, above all, was a teacher of values, and *Pilgrimage to the Rebirth* is an example of what he taught. The manuscript represents his dedication to the unconscious and sets forth his role, as the first son of God, in receiving the Light of Aquarius and carrying it into consciousness. Only history will determine the degree of his success.

Theodore Young

Acknowledgments

Gratefully, I have accepted the help of many, but those who follow are very special to me.

THEO E. YOUNG came several summers in succession to Zürich to help distill out of my unconscious the full story of the Pilgrimage, which I had written in my diary in an almost skeleton form. His great contribution is that he insisted on my own style and forced me into further clarifications.

In Zürich, I received much encouragement from my Jungian friends ANIELA JAFFÉ and CORNELIA BRUNNER as well as the Drs. YECHESKEL and RIWKAH KLUGER from Haifa.

In Oxford, Dr. MARGARET WILEY MARSHALL was very helpful with some early editing. She and her late husband, Dr. RODERICK MARSHALL, have been very supportive of my myth.

OLIVIER BERNIER was of great help with his typing and keen observations. ANDOR BRAUN, who undertook the design and shepherded this book through the presses, had a scrutinizing eye for "le mot juste," for which I am most grateful.

It seems so appropriate that the owners of an old American priory, TOM and HARRIE SCHLOSS, are responsible for a most thoughtful and generous financial arrangement. Last but not least, it is IRINA PABST, on the board of Wainwright House in Rye, N.Y., who helped to smooth the way so that this outstanding institution of the humanities and Jungian thought could be the support behind this publication.

To all my friends, again, my heartfelt thanks.

Erlo van Waveren

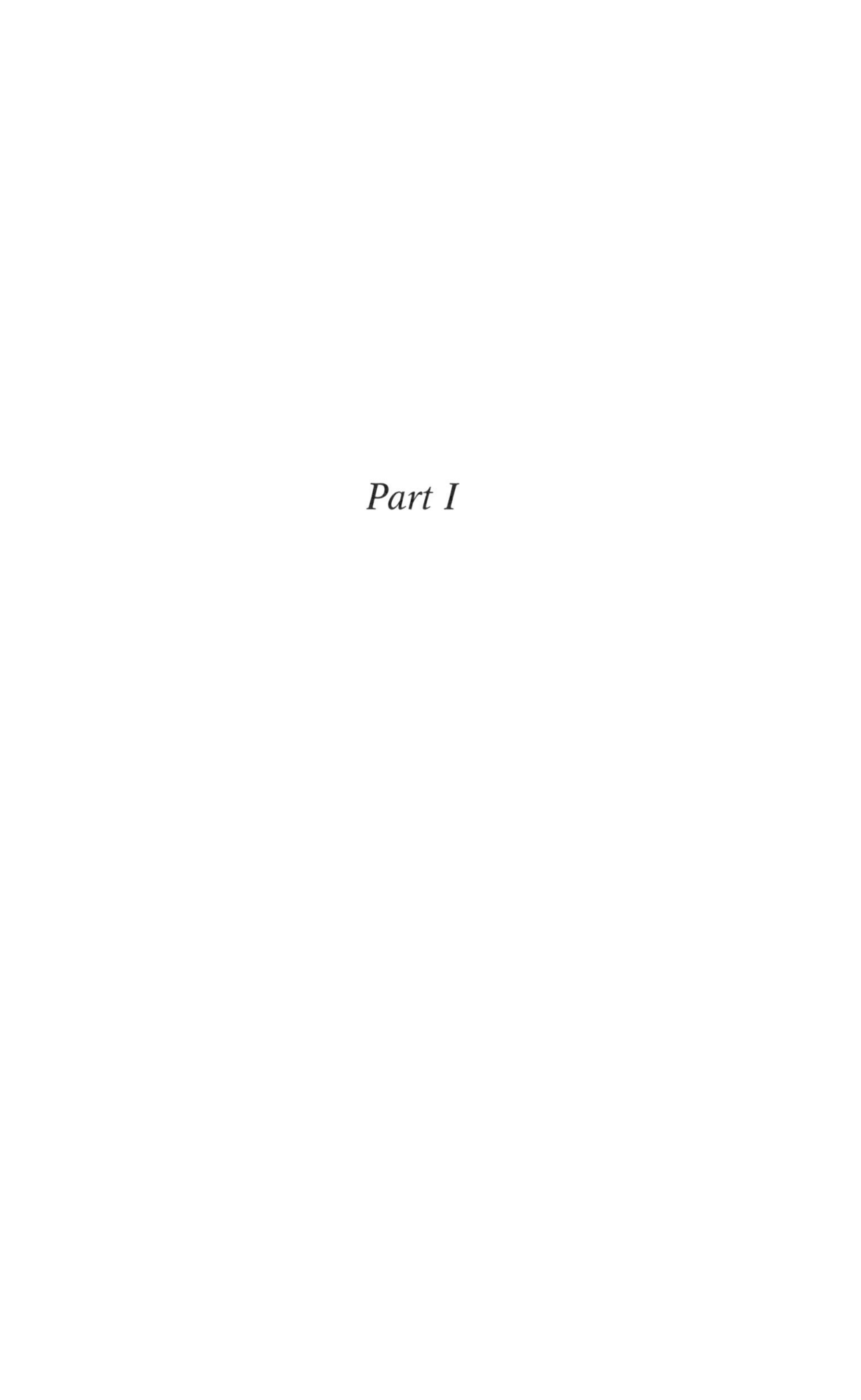

Part I

Foreword

Though my husband and I have accepted the fact that there are mysteries in life that cannot be explained, but must just be accepted, we were still unprepared for the revelations in this book. They were received at times with incredulity and awe, but never denied. For many years, however, we kept them to ourselves, never expecting to place them before the public eye. But life often brings about an unexpected demand.

Reincarnation is an important aspect of this book. We had accepted reincarnation as a probability, but had never liked loose and easy talk about past lives, believing always that this present life, fully lived, is the one of importance. Hence we had never attempted to explore our past lives. It was thus with the greatest shock of surprise that we were forced to give our attention to them.

Nor did my husband ever expect to write a book about those lives. However, as he reveals, he was forced to keep a record, and this volume is the result. It is in the form of a myth, his myth, as it were. All of us carry a myth, life's splendid tale lived out in us, whether we know it or not. Since time immemorial, people have spun legends and myths, symbolic tales that hold a truth impossible to express in everyday words. One's own myth is the story of a psychic truth which we are living; sometimes too harsh to take literally, but nevertheless true and laden with meaning. It is the journey of the soul. That journey has meaning not only for the individual, but for others as well.

This book is based upon dreams and visions, both of which have been rather suspect since the Reformation. But in ancient times, it was taken for granted that dreams and visions contained important meanings – and again in this century, they seem to be gaining in importance. These meanings have been interpreted by special persons with insight into such phenomena. The medicine man, or shaman, was a well known and deeply revered figure, and still is in certain cultures. It is not just in the Bible that we have records of dreams. In Roman history, there are the well recorded dreams of Scipio, Hannibal and Caesar; in Plato, we have a record of Socrates' dreams. Lincoln's prophetic dream just before his assassination is known in American history. Religious literature is full of the dreams and visions of saints and mystics. Visions, too, have great importance. They appear, in a waking state, often as symbols, and should be interpreted as one would interpret a dream.

There is much talk at the present time about the Aquarian Age. Our earth is constantly moving through the twelve signs of the Zodiac. It takes about two thousand years for the earth to move through each sign, and as we approach the end of the sign of Pisces, we enter the sign of Aquarius: the Aquarian Age. Each sign has its peculiar symbolism, which seems to be reflected in the civilization and religion of that era. For instance, Pisces is the sign of the Fishes, and the fish is important as a Christian symbol. Fish live in the water, and often swim in schools. Hence groups were important in the Piscean Age. Organizations flourished.

With the waning of an era, great changes take place, and there is much disruption. The old is receding into the past; the new is not yet stabilized and evident. The old consciousness is becoming the basis for the new. The old concept of Christianity is slipping over the horizon of consciousness, to become the fertilizing factor in the new Age of Aquarius. The symbol of the Aquarian sign is the Waterman, who holds a jar containing the waters of life. An individual consciousness is now required, which forms that container, and we can no longer live unconsciously like a fish.

One change that is already appearing in the world is the prominence of the dark side of life: evil, we call it. In Christianity, the black fish was suppressed as much as possible and only the white fish was accepted. The water jar of Aquarius, however, contains a wholeness that was not present in Pisces. Black and white are both there, intermingled. No longer can the black remain hidden and unredeemed. Both are in life. The consciousness of the individual must provide the resolution. That is the task for the Aquarian Age.

The casual reader who picks up this volume may find it totally irrelevant to the realities of life today, especially if he tries to approach life on a completely rational basis. But another type of reader, searching for something out of the ordinary trend of thought, with a mind open to the irrational side of life, will find it both revealing and illuminating.

Ann van Waveren

Prologue

This book is written out of the pain of the inner man. I belong to those who have been forced to travel a road of self-awareness and, in doing so, I have had to become better acquainted with the Self, that composite nucleus which holds my very essence. Not everybody has to make the journey I have logged here. I offer this tale to those whose need for inner contact has made itself known.

This inner journey is an ancient road. Thousands upon thousands have had to face the realities of the spirit knowingly, but millions upon millions have trod the same road without realizing where they were going or what was happening to them.

The language of this road is always symbolic: the directions are seldom received in direct communication.

My travels through the ages past, my contacts with my inner signposts, my angels, my Christ, the symbols of Aquarius and of the Piscean Age, the divine language of the deep layers of the unconscious, all have come to me through words I often could not comprehend until I became aware that ancestral psychic components were compelling me to write a song – a song of divine and human beings, a song of agony and delight, a song of opposites in which one would balance the other.

My outer life seldom reflected these so-called poetic times. What storms were raging in my inner being! How I had to bend and buckle under those immense unconscious forces! They were unconscious at first; but slowly, as they jousted with my ego, I came to understand their purpose and to realize that this was a symbolic quest.

They told me a story of change, a story of the endless changes of life, a story of death and rebirth. I became aware of the cosmic paths of our sun through the Houses of the Zodiac, and how, with that cosmic rotation, our Sun-God has to go through his evolution in order to experience through man the changes inherent in his own Being.

In this endless round of change, on the wheel of life, I found myself bound – bound tightly to the cosmic changes and the consequent personal changes in my own poor, limited mind.

I suffered, I groaned, but relentlessly the great Song of my Soul kept pounding its rhythms in the almost incomprehensible language of the symbol.

So here I give you the Song of my Soul. I hope it will not be too painful. Perhaps you are my companion on this road; perhaps the story of this symbolic journey through my inner being is just what you need. Then you are not so alone and, for a moment, we will sing a duet, you, my reader, and I, and then silently, we will go each our own way. But you will know that somewhere there is a kindred soul who could, like a scribe, write down God's language, Soul language. And then you may understand what this song of mine is about, in spite of the many mysteries that will remain hidden from both of us.

Be willing to read the well nigh incomprehensible pilgrimage of a wayfarer in the land of his ancestors. I pray that it may bring us into a companionship – even though we may not know each other.

As this book goes out to unknown hands, I reveal my innermost agonies and delights. Guard these precious jewels well and share their worth with those you love, as deep within my heart, I love you. I give you this secret, which I have kept hidden even from myself – until today.

A Necessary Introduction

> "The dream is a little hidden door in the innermost and most secret recesses of the psyche, opening into that cosmic night which was psyche long before there was an ego consciousness and which will remain psyche no matter how far our ego consciousness may extend."
>
> C. G. Jung[1]

In 1955, I dreamed that the Buddha appeared through a round hole – the Breathing Hole of Eternity –, stepped on the foot of my bed and then onto the floor, where he seated himself in the Lotus position. He communicated the thought that I was to seat myself in his lap and spray my semen in the form of a peacock's tail on his chest.

This dream is the unexpected demand which my wife refers to in her introduction. To me, the Buddha is a world spirit of enfolding and divine consciousness, capable of human existence. The request of that great power has been the driving force behind this revelation of my innermost being. The peacock's tail is found on many ancient tombs as a sign of rebirth.

But it all started in 1945. My wife and I were spending the weekend on the beautiful estate of Meudon on the north shore of Long Island. As I look back, it seems a long, long time ago. The estate is now Lattingtown Village. Some of our friends and acquaintances presently live facing the greenhouse gardens, another lives in the groom's house, and our oldest friend resides with her family in the butler's cottage by the small

[1] C.G. Jung, *Memories, Dreams, Reflections*. Vintage Books, New York, 1965, p. 382.

pond still there. We have all grown considerably older – and I hope wiser – since then.

I will never forget that weekend. We were staying with our friends in the groom's house, which was charmingly and simply rebuilt. The warm hospitality of our hostess, the long walks on the beach and in the woods thrust us deep in ourselves. On Monday morning, we would go back to the big city. It was in the night from Sunday to Monday that I had the Great Dream which started a new chapter in my life, bringing with it a life full of loneliness and secrecy.

I awoke that Monday morning between three and four with a terrifying shock. I had dreamed that I was on my way to primary school in my home town of Haarlem, in Holland. I was not a young schoolboy in my dream, but my own age, in the early forties. The streets were all exactly the way they still are in that old city. At the crossroads, just before the block on which my school was located, there appeared out of the sky a great fatherly figure, his head faintly outlining the sturdy contours of my father's skull. I did not see any particular features. However, I knew right away that this was a manifestation of the Godhead, – still, I called him Father Time. His legs never showed – only his immense torso and face. He stretched out his arm, right or left, I don't remember exactly – more likely the left arm – and blessed me, making the sign of the Cross. Automatically, I raised my right arm and blessed him, and while making the sign of the Cross to Him, I noticed that I had in my hand a dishmop, the kind I still use in the kitchen to wash dishes. The next moment, I was transported to the other side of life, and for an infinitesimal time, I was in the world of the dead. I felt no pain, but just the same I wept and shrieked out in agony. Again, a sudden shift in my dream brought me back to the street, and, there at the crossroads, invisible hands put me in a blue serge suit, which was rather tight on me and chafed slightly under my arms. I protested to the Heavenly Father that He changed my clothing without asking me if I wanted it changed or if I liked it. There was no answer from Him. Then He blocked the way to my school and pointed towards my right, where the old narrow streets lead to the middle of the town, the marketplace.

I woke up in sheer terror. The power of this visionary dream shook me to the bottom of my soul. I knew that I would die. I had seen the face of God. I had been in His shattering presence. It was of no help to me that the night before I had dreamt of the same street, crowded with people, carrying candles in their hands. They were celebrating a service which, for a short moment, had transported me to the land of the dead.

I got out of bed; though I am in the habit of recording my dreams, it didn't even occur to me to write this one down. Instead, I started to write my last will in the back of my dream book. In large letters, I wrote so it could not be overlooked, ever. My life would finish, if not that day then soon after. The shock was such that I didn't even tell the dream to my wife or speak of my apprehension. As Jungian analysts, my wife and I always tell each other our dreams, and our notebooks are, to this day, next to our beds.

On the way to New York City, I expected a crash. I didn't stop praying during the entire trip of one hour and a half. But nothing happened on that beautiful spring morning. We both saw our clients in the afternoon, and by dinnertime, I had enough courage, still being alive, to tell my wife that I needed to speak to.her about a startling dream of the early morning.

So after dinner, we sat in our little green room, named after the dark green walls the former owner had ingeniously decorated. I started to speak slowly and hesitantly, for the moment I put my attention to the content of my dream, I was aware again of an awe in me towards that Heavenly Figure – St. Augustine's experience led him to write about "a spiritual force which the mind was unable to grasp."

All my life I had been forced by circumstances not to follow the academic path. Finances were never the trouble, but emotionally, I was unsuited and too heavily burdened by my complexes to pursue an academic career. Also, my powerful father always wished me to become a merchant and not a doctor like his brother, although that would have been my mother's choice. So when Father Time blocked my way to school, I readily recognized that as a pattern of my life. Professor Jung, who advised several of my confrères to become doctors, never suggested that road to me. Neither did he ever ask about my studies, which were mostly done in my later teens with private tutors. In my early twenties, I traveled to several countries where there were branches of the family business; hence my stay in America.

But why, now, this dream? Why call God the Father, Father Time? For that question stuck very much in my memory. Why that sedate blue suit, which was binding under my arms? Why those blessings? All these questions were not answered until much later. That night, in the little green room, deeply under the influence of the confrontation, I started to philosophize about my life – the different road I had traveled from that of my mercantile brothers, and the great decision, after my father's death, to leave the family business and to start out for myself. That was a totally fresh and new idea to me, so different from the semi-feudal background in which I had been forced to follow the family tradition.

After a while, I stretched out on the sofa and, traveling further into myself, I began to understand more about my future life. My breathing became deeper and deeper and directed my thought world. I became aware of having a task in life, a destiny all my own, dictated by something within me – the soul, or perhaps the Self, to use a Jungian term for our totality. I found myself telling Ann the purpose of both my present and former life as naturally as if I had been gossiping over a cup of tea. I remember one sentence clearly when, with real humor, my inner voice first bemusedly told my wife, "Well, we could have found perhaps a better one" – and then, addressing itself to me, said, "but you will do."

Because of this voice which spoke from rock bottom, I was firmly convinced that in my former life I had been a teacher of life's values and had returned to continue in that work. I had not solved the message of the dream, but I knew that a greater force in me was now directing my personal life, and that my own ego and personality would have to learn a few things to adjust. I realized that I was on a new, rather constricted, road which at the same time was the continuation of an old one. Then I sat up, punch drunk and still deep within myself.

With the catalytic curiosity of a true wife, Ann asked me naturally and oh, so calmly, "But have you any idea who you were?" And just as calmly "it" spoke right through me and I said "Fénelon." I was stunned, and could have been knocked over with a feather. Ann, not quite remembering his name, asked, "Who is he?" So I looked in the encyclopedia to refresh my memory. While she went to the kitchen to make me a hot drink, I started to read about this French archbishop, a rather controversial figure at the court of Louis XIV. Towards the end of the essay, I became emotionally so upset that I slammed the book shut. Direct memory and a highly charged state of consciousness took over, and I experienced the deep emotions which Fénelon had not been able to assimilate at the beginning of the eighteenth century. I paced the room and, stopping in front of the bookcase, I pointed towards the line of encyclopedias and said: "Before Fénelon, I was Lord Gray, with an a or an e, and he is hidden in those books, too."

After calming down with my warm drink and recovering my everyday senses, I said to my wife: "Well, what this all means, I don't know. I will have to look at my dreams to explain this, and to find out whether it is all an emotional projection and a psychological truth or an actual fact." For eleven years I had been analyzed and was analyzing myself. Our yearly trips to Zürich before World War II to work with Professor Jung and listen to his private seminars as well as his university lectures, had played an immense role in our lives, and we are still deeply dependent on our dreams to show us the real state of affairs.

So that night, I went to bed feeling rather skeptical about my eternal world, reincarnation, and being in the grip of ancient memories. Nevertheless I was undeniably impressed by the power and emotional content of an inner experience so foreign to me. My dreams would have to tell me how to accept this baffling revelation – and they did.

The next morning, on awakening, I had the confirmation. That night I had dreamt that I was being led first into an oriental chamber. A leather ball was placed on the floor right at the entrance. I gave it a firm kick, very reminiscent of my boyhood soccer days, and the ball hit smack in the middle of a gong, a bull's-eye shot. I can still remember the vibrating sound, sonorous, full and round, as if the entire world should hear it. Then I was brought to the Hall of Justice, situated at right angles to the Oriental section. I entered into an atmosphere of profound truth and integrity, where no law of nature could be trespassed. Several people sat on benches and were listening as my most rational, mercantile, worldly brother tried to sunder his relationship with his newly acquired fiancée.

The judge was seated on a raised paneled platform, listening to my brother, who was trying to get back the diamond he had given his future wife. The judge refused the request. The marriage had to take place. Thus my most rational side had to accept the new link with the unconscious; an alliance had to be made, and the stunning revelations of the night before accepted. Then the judge raised his right arm and pointed at nine more diamonds suspended in mid air, representing, with their different sizes and intensities of brilliance, nine former lives with which my most worldly side, as well as my spiritual side, had to get acquainted. With another flash, there appeared the diamond representing my present life. At that I awoke in turmoil.

What a rebellion there was in my twentieth-century, civilized, sophisticated being. In fact, such was my resistance that when, a few weeks later, a dream started to refer to another life of mine, I swung my arms wildly in my sleep and broke through the dream world into my daily consciousness. My only memory was that it was another bishop whose name started with a "W." Several weeks after that, I dreamed of a fern with five stalks, representing five bishop's crosiers. They were growing right at the corner of our house in the country. So I was in for it; serious and troublesome times lay ahead of me.

At that time, Cary Baynes, the translator of the English edition of the *I Ching* and her sister, Mrs. Henri Zinno, were the only friends in whom my wife and I dared to confide. We were in deep isolation, even from our own psychological world.

Five years later, in 1950, I spoke with Professor Jung about these surprising developments. In our conversation, he was as open, frank and revelatory as he would ever be with me. Our discussion then was at such an intimate level that the next day he requested Mrs. Jung to speak to me at the Jung Institute and tell me not to talk to anyone about our conversation. In our Western world, Eastern concepts are often sooner accepted when presented in a more or less scientific light. Professor Jung was a past master at that. Whenever he spoke to me about an incarnation, it was referred to as an ancestor; "ancestral components," "psychic ancestors," "ancestral souls" are all expressions which Professor Jung used to express the idea of metamorphosis with which I am dealing in this book.

Through my dreams, I became aware of the ancestral heritage of my present day life. I visited many of the places connected with my psychic components, which was most interesting, but trying at times. Curiously enough, those visits integrated my "characters" very much into the Now of my present-day, twentieth-century self.

In *Memories, Dreams, Reflections* Professor Jung writes:

> "It had been asked by, as it were, my spiritual forefathers in the hope and expectation that they would learn what they had not been able to find out during their time on earth, since the answers first had to be created in the centuries that followed.... If question and answer had already been in existence in eternity, had always been there, no effort on my part would have been necessary and it could all have been discovered in any other century. There does seem to be unlimited knowledge

present in nature, it is true, but it can be comprehended by consciousness only when the time is ripe for it."[1]

For me, that time is now. To paraphrase Paul, who lived nearly 2000 years ago: "The trumpet shall sound, and the dead shall be raised, incorruptible; we shall not die."

It has taken twenty centuries, but now it can be written with conviction that the dead can return incorruptible to the state of consciousness they had in past centuries and continue their psychic awareness now and in future ages. Indeed, time is not.

The manifestation of God as Father Time in the dream is for me a sign that my unconscious wants me to be aware of the changing times in the Godhead. The Piscean Age of Christian endeavor is drawing to its close and is making way for the Age of Aquarius.

[1] C.G. Jung, *Memories, Dreams, Reflections*, p. 307.

December 14, 1968
New York City
11:30 p.m.

Never, never in my life had I thought I would write intimately about my psychic experiences. At times, all hell broke loose in my poor brain, and never, never had I thought that my turbulent psyche would want me to be exposed to the views of unknown people. I have lived a life hidden and unknown except to a few, a very few who often would soon forget the unorthodox part of my life; so that I would again appear as just another handsome gentleman and happy husband of distinguished background.

Now my Lord, my Self, you force me to bring to light my sojourn through this life, with the accidents and happenings of a soul most willing to hide what it knows. I fear that terribly. Why do you torture me out of my hiding, oh Lord? Why make me a spectacle to attract the present-day contempt of the so-called educated people? Why, now, the glare of daylight? Give me the darkness of the unknown, where I am safe and away from jealous dragons, hungry for the gold born of the pain of my tear-torn and trampled ego! Why can't I stay hidden so that I can soothe the last scars which hide the gashes? Why can't I wait until my skin safely covers my wounds? Power, power of the Unknown, why force me out into the open, away from the privacy of my own suffering, bearable only through the sweet love of my wife?

Oh, but I cry in vain, my voice is not heard, or it is heard and not heeded. Or is it heard, and smoothly and relentlessly put aside for a greater issue? Is the story again, as before, and now, and ever after, the sacrifice of the one for the many? Haven't I learned that lesson? Haven't I learned and listened to that ancient song of the human soul: one shall lead, and those who love will follow in his path? Is it my path to open the black wounds of darkness for the thousands of seekers? If so, where, oh Lord, is your ointment? Where is your healing salve? Will humanity suffer unto eternity? Is that why I now bring to the blinking eyes of the many my innermost secrets and happenings? This is a lament, not from the heart alone, not just from the head or feet. It is a lament from all of me, who in the outer world am Erlo van Waveren, born in Hillegom, Holland, son of the bulb merchant, Theodoor and his wife, Marie, from Amsterdam.

Tears, tears, but to no effect. Steadily, like a drumbeat slowly pulsating from distances far, far away in cosmic silence born comes the Word:

"Erlo, Erlo, bare yourself for your own protection. Help, help those who, like you, have suffered in darkness and do not know why. You have suffered the psychic pain of your eternal existence. You have been made aware of a consciousness in the Eternal Light. Darkness, with its deeper shadows, and its mystery and mysterious forebodings, has taught you a priceless lesson. Shine, shine, star of darkness and of light, unknown yet to those who go about groping, seeking, seeking everywhere for that which is *theirs* – their God, their Redeemer, their Self – sensed, surmised, but not as yet experienced.

"You know. You know for yourself concretely what has been the path of your experiences. They don't. They do not know. Their peculiar ways lead them astray in a world of rational miasma, and their souls go begging for an answer.

"Now start your record, as calmly and clearly as possible, about your dream life, and the life you have forced yourself to live as a well-camouflaged seeker. A fool of God you are, but not of man. Write about your psychic life and the wonders it has brought you. From afar, the drums and trumpets are sounding the hour of revelation of your myth, so that God and man may judge.

"Don't ever try to be understood. Don't ever try to achieve. Don't address any particular group of people. Tell your story, for if it is left untold, disaster will follow. This is not a threat, it is a truth. Tell your story to the tribe because the happenings of your life are too burdensome to be carried alone. Share it according to true American Indian tradition. Now go to bed, it is past midnight."

The next morning

The snow has covered all the ugliness of our dirty town. The garden looks immaculately white, and I am seated in the living-room overlooking the pretty picture of our small snowscape. What a relief it is not to work today! The chores have been done, and I will now try to write as simply as possible.

Many strange bedfellows have come my way. They were attracted to me by a bond I wish I didn't have. In dreams, in dreamlike states, against my protests, they came out of darkness, revealing themselves in order to make me aware of a psychic state that was apparently waiting for clarification. It seems as if in my psyche nothing can come to rest until consciousness is capable of experiencing it with feeling and emotion. Painfully, these ancestors of my soul worked themselves into my fantasy world to take on different aspects of their characters, returning to life in this book to become reborn and integrated into this new age of Aquarius. Never, never had they thought to come back and live unlived, unresolved regions of their psyche. But Aquarius came, and Gabriel sounded his trumpet and loudly announced the coming of the New Age, even unto the Netherworlds.

Paul, in his first Epistle to the Corinthians, is just as profound and true now as two thousand years ago when he prophesied to his faraway flock: "Behold, I show you a mystery; we shall not all sleep, but we shall be changed, in a moment, in the twinkling of an eye, at the last trumpet: for the trumpet shall sound and the dead shall be raised incorruptible and we shall be changed."

Now the trumpets are being raised and their call heard by the living and the dead. And so my psychic ancestors came to me. It is as Paul wrote to his Corinthians: "For this corruptible must put on incorruption and this mortal must put on immortality."

In curious formation they came, like diamonds in a row. I saw them, involved in the resurrection of Jerusalem, no richer or truer city ever existed. To Jerusalem, the City of God, the seat of our eternal being, they went to undergo the revivification of their spirit. Through much travail they came. First through my psyche, then through the tale they spun with their magic lives, they brought to light the new spirit of Aquarius in me.

Aroused by the mane of the times, Wilfrid, the saint of York, the archbishop of the seventh century, came out of his grave. He had to become aware of what he had destroyed in primitive man of those ancient days in his beloved England by establishing Roman rule and ritual at the council of Whitby in 664. At that time, the beauty of England's pre-Christian spirit was violated and its wild naturalness was thrown into the pit of Hell under the altar of his Church. The civilized ritual of greater sophistication, based on the marvelous Gregorian spirit of Italy, was superimposed on those pagan children, to the greater glory of God and to the delight of Hell. For centuries to come, this darkening of pagan lights, this "cover-up" of Nature's magic, would create fierce battles in the Christian psyche which now have to be released, depotentiated and reinstalled as a vital, positive life-force. So Aquarius awakened Saint Wilfrid in the North Riding of York to make his pilgrimage into consciousness.

For the same reasons, and according to the laws of the Eternal Return, my spiritual ancestors reappeared to seek clarification of that which could not be lived or understood before by the limitations of their times and their incarnations. Thus appeared the powerful Walter de Gray, Archbishop of York from 1216 to 1255; the sophisticated François de Fénelon, Archbishop of Cambrai from 1695 to 1715; the undaunted Saint Asterius, Archbishop of Amasia, who lived the entire length of the fourth century, initiating the adoration of relics, and who wrote homilies that would again be much read five centuries later. My first Christian ancestor is Judas Barsabas, a prophet in his own right, and brother of the candidate for the place of Judas Iscariot. These men are my spiritual forefathers.

Then there is Kerl, an old Dutch word for the common man. I call him Kerel – the Lord Kyros. Kyros means Lord or master, so I take Kerel, Carl, Karel, Karoll, Charles as derivatives of the word Kyros, meaning, to me, the Lord Man. In my writing, he represents all that man has ever lived through in our human experience. He is an aspect of the wise man, the one who knows all that has been lived. Kerel is the archetypal man in us all, that fount of information available to us when we are willing and able to listen.

The Hotel Schloss Ragaz
Bad Ragaz, Switzerland
July 27, 1966

The event of my birth is hidden from me in a twilight zone. It is not all darkness to me, not the black of the total unknown. It seems rather that I can recall faintly a terrific pull and attraction to Mother Earth, as if in the hidden crevices of tissues and sinews there would be for me a light of unknown beauty. My soul cried out in an agony of delight: "Make the plunge." This cry forced me to dive, and with a thundering crash of lightning, I came through that mysterious wall which separates the worlds. I was born.

The experiences of the other side seemed removed. I was now enclosed in a box of feeling-flesh, sensitive to everything but aware of nothing except the moment of separation from all I knew, all I remembered of another universe of endless possibilities and bewildering vistas. I was caught by the Lord's call, which had catapulted me into this world with enormous power and will, and I was received by Earth with an equally powerful element of love. It seemed that the creative and the receptive, two all-important powers, had bound me to a giant shuttlecock, embedding me in the great design being woven in this cosmos.

At that moment of entrance, a terrible sense of bewilderment overcame me, a chaotic moment in which all my values had to be realigned. My gravity became my body: my thoughts lost their power as if their wings had been clipped by a giant scissor. My mind twirled and twisted. It was as if my new body of flesh was now my only freedom. My spirit gave a desperate yell, which penetrated this new-found freedom as my very essence sensed the oncoming agony of being encased in a mortal body. The birth had succeeded.

Here I was on earth, catapulted, attracted, received, expected, in agony and bewildered, but seemingly full of purpose and obeying a thousand and one reactions and animal complexes, the greatest of which was love, good warm animal love of the mother body. Without that love, the entire miracle of my coming would have ended in a dark hole of blackness, despair and death. The impact of birth, with its enormous archaic powers and rituals, its vast complicated laws, and deep, gripping emotions, was completely dependent on one factor. Could all this immensity be received and carried by the love of my mother? Not just the mother's love for the powers of life working through her, but love for my particular individual soul making its entrance into the world.

Three days later
on July 30
in Bad Ragaz

With my birth I had painfully broken the ties of love in a world of the beyond in order to establish my new being here on earth, to start a new cycle, a new beginning in the endless chain of Being. In one way, there would be no difference, for I live wherever I am. On the other hand, there was this immense new undertaking of returning. I was reborn in a new body, a new opportunity to mend the old ills and fears, and provide a new alive consciousness with which to continue the eternal round of living. After every dive into this earthly life, a new, more challenging beginning for the life hereafter is established. Then, as this new awareness on the other side becomes devitalized by its use, a return is made, a new descent into this world so that we may achieve the next goal in our eternal rounds. To experience, to fight, to become, to leave, and to return to this unique earth of ours is what the immense spirit of man needs and wants. For nothing is more vitalizing, nothing more rewarding to the soul than the apparent, but not actual, mire of our earthly experience. In this place of dense psyche, which is our earth, and with the *Prima Materia,* we live, we play, we manipulate, we experiment in order to find the light of consciousness. It is not to find out who we are, that matters, but *what* we are as human beings. Who we are is the mystery, perhaps gradually unveiled by what we are.

I feel that a myth is being evolved, as if the dreamer in me wanted to tell an ancient tale of the soul. I know from experience that the knowledge of the unconscious will voice truths which seem strange to the rational mind. However, if I refuse to accept these ideas, a part of my nature will be cut off.

In any case, I have no choice; so I might as well stop fighting. Those ideas, those voices seek expression.

We are now in the Engadine Valley
in Sils Maria, the place Nietzsche so loved
It is August 3

A strong inner voice speaks:

"The greatest difficulty, my dear Erlo, is your worldliness, a curious combination of several factors which was clearly shown to you in this morning's dream. It is absolutely necessary to give up the ego expression, and even the soul has to be pure of heart in order to receive the message of what Aquarius wants you to know. Your personal expression will come automatically because it is the only way you can receive the universal message which is now constantly beamed out and is responsible for your conflict. The old cannot comprehend the new. Now try to be that quality, that spirit you are, but without the peculiarities of the twentieth century. The material, rational world of today has to be thoroughly understood in order to be discarded. You are still trying to cut a figure in it as a psychologist or a writer with a masterwork to perform. However, let it be performed through you, whatever it is, and do not interfere with what I shall create. I am that Mystery beyond Time, beyond human comprehension, not to be defined. Call me the Voice, the Self, the Void, Eros or Logos, or whatever you will – but do not ignore me. Give up the world and love me as the true source of that which is, was, and is to be. Now, write your farewell to the world, and try to do it tomorrow."

The next day
August 4
Sils Maria

About my writing:

Before any serious work is attempted, I must bid farewell to all that is in my world, even to my psychology of life. My twentieth century wall has to tumble. It is a death, a complete death which is involved. Can I ever do it? I will walk in the woods now, not alone, but with my darling wife, Ann.

On August 5
in Sils Maria
I wrote:

The Good-bye

Lord, help me! Once before, I said good-bye to my ego expression. It was perhaps the greatest agony I have ever experienced. I had worked hard and looked forward to a stage career, when my dreams indicated that I was a psychologist. The struggle to dare to be an actor had been so difficult after giving up the directorships of two old family concerns. Now, by writing this book, I know I must give up my own ideas regarding my contribution to psychology. I have been successful in it for so many years. People have trusted me, and I have been deeply devoted to helping those who came for advice. I had always hoped to do something in the world of my peers, to write a book, to teach or lecture; thus I would have given my contribution to the world of psychology and to the world of my friends. But now I say good-bye to this. That kind of ego satisfaction shall not be mine.

I also wanted acclaim from the world, and from the people who are making important contributions to this age. But good-bye to that, as well. Good-bye to all my ego wishes for the admiration, affection and respect of my dear and beloved friends. All that is still animal vanity, like the pride of the wolf with a glossy coat. I go to a different land now, not by choice, but by life's will. Otherwise nothing can grow in me any more, even with the love and support of those nearest to me. I have to travel on, not further away, but deeper into a life I have not as yet experienced on earth.

For me, the difficulty of going on is the fact that I seem to leave behind a world in which I am not allowed to make my mark. I feel like a wayfarer who travels towards a goal but will always be a stranger to it. No one knows of me, and I have to leave my own circle before fulfillment. Nobody will know that I have lived, and no lasting product of my ego existence will be allowed.

But now my inner voice says: "It is not just a matter of giving up what you love. It is rather an uprooting of what you thought you could and really should accomplish. Even your psychic ancestors will never notice your worth until after the sacrifice of your ego. Before your expression is fulfilled, death comes."

Then where I will go is not important; it is beyond my comprehension. I fear to go into the oblivion, like Isaiah the Second. No one knows who he was; only what came through him. Through his sufferings, he extracted a universal truth to be used for ages to come. But can I stand such pain? Is my soul willing to go that road?

Where will I go and what will happen to me? I don't know, and it seems very unimportant. My death is all that matters, the death of my worldly knowledge as well as my spiritual knowledge. Ego and spirit are both at stake. The crucifixion must be complete – the death of any wish for expression, absolute. All this comes out of the deep conviction that nothing further can develop in me unless my ego – my brain, my mind, my ambition – all know and realize that Erlo as such is nonproductive and unimportant. Almost sixty-four years of effort, undonc?

Now my inner being speaks: "Good-bye, my dear Erlo, good-bye. Oh, so many thanks for your efforts. I love your ambitions and all of your vanities. But please, please, oh please, do not come back! For if you return, all suffering is in vain. Your life, such as it was, would only turn into poisonous dust instead of the rock which it can become. This is true even if your life remains but a stepping stone for unknown feet, like the life of Isaiah the Second, the beautiful Egyptian known only to you and to me and remembered with the deepest love and affection." At this moment, I feel that I want a big, beautifully carved scarab over my heart and on my hand in remembrance of his life.

Now once again I have to disappear and enter into a development which entails my death.

"Die, Erlo! Go to your death with my tears as a blessing and my thanks. Go into oblivion, and leave all your desires and wishes. Drop them as a tree sheds its leaves so only that which is immortal remains. I know, you have but faint interest in immortality. That which is mortal tastes of this earth, which you did not know you loved so much. Have no desire left – be empty – be nothing – and see what happens. Walk in life as if you were an empty framework but pray to Heaven that the Devil does not enter; nor should there be any desires for the entrance of the Great."

With tears streaming down my face, and completely numbed by the total identification with my inner voice, I wrote the above.

Then the reaction came. The unknown will have to make a mighty proposition before I can continue on my task with any love or devotion. Life ahead is a vacuum, a Void, and that is needed, I suppose.

August 7, 1966
Sils Maria

You don't dare to give in to the greater idea, do you, Erlo? When you went to sleep, I told you, you are your own Redeemer. But, no, you knew better. You wake up and your heart is beating too fast. Still, you are the Redeemer. But, no, Erlo knows better. No one will descend for you. You are your own descent and ascent, your own Christ, your own Self. In you lies your own Redemption and Resurrection into self awareness and consciousness.

"The Redeemer is too great? Who or what else can there be but your own star, your own inner light. Is there a greater principle? Is there anyone else *now,* in the flesh, who could take on the role?

"Accept! Accept and find peace."

"Who cares who is the Redeemer? If I am, it will show. If I'm not, it will show. Foolishness of the unconscious. If my heart beats that much and is not at rest, tell me what it is I fight....

"Well, then, I will not fight the idea of the Redeemer. Fine. That is it. I am. Then all anxiety can leave, for I have nothing to do any more; the Redeemer will have to live through me....

"So I let go. Everything is fine. Erlo – *niente.* Redeemer is It. As you see, I am indifferent. But rest does not come to me. Perhaps in a while I will stop fighting the idea altogether. I will accept it from simple exhaustion, I suppose....

"Is there still no relief? Well, then, I accept that I am, but what I am has to be proven. Perhaps this, perhaps that. I accept. But now, of course, you want me to accept the idea with love and warmth and human equilibrium."

"Erlo! Erlo! Erlo! You must realize that the spirit of the Redeeming Self is so great that it can write and speak the words of Christ and Buddha. These words brought light and comfort to the world. When the Redeemer is accepted and is alive in you, then the World Anima calls, and gods and ancestors claim their own."

"I realize that. But what within me fights it?"

"You'd never guess! Dress now, go out on the mountain; but walk slowly, and return to your room."

I did dress and walked through the beautiful larch woods of the Engadine, then came back to the hotel. And when I sat at my window, the following came:

"There is an entire Christian system of monks, priests, bishops and archbishops who are rebelling. They want to continue what was; they do not want to change. They were all so good, so hardworking, so insistent on Christian ways that you ought to talk to them, for they are all in an uproar. Their work is over and they hate it, but they have to be redeemed in order to be pillars of life's wisdom in the age to come. The pre-Christians within you don't bother you. The Christians do, and give you a terrible time, for they know that now they have to die and be reborn in you and they were so deliciously self-satisfied with their jobs."

August 8, 1966
Sils Maria

Well, my dear old Christian ancestors, where are you? Fénelon, what is still on your mind, and my dear old scrappy Wilfrid, what is on yours? You two, and perhaps Judas Barsabas, are most perturbed. Asterius is happy because he can always participate in deep emotion, and Walter de Gray knows enough about the darkness of life not to be too delighted with Christianity. Asterius, will you come to my help? Wilfrid will be most upset because he loved and established the Roman Church in his England, and all his work has to be changed.

But now I hear Wilfrid's voice clearly, coming through all possible barriers. It is almost gruff and irritated.

"Arouse! Arouse! I hear it clearly. The trumpet sounds. I hear it, the trumpet, I hear it. Aroused I am, by your crude new spirit. Watch out! What harvest will that bring you: you disturb my beatitude, my soothing, healing influences, bringing peace and hope in a world of scandalous attitudes and vulgar behavior. Why arouse me from the deep, benevolent sleep of my sainthood, from which I dispense my blessings to all who want to follow the spirit of the Lord Christ?"

I keep silent. I realize that the silence creates unrest in Wilfrid's aroused spirit. Then he continues:

"Is this the end of time for which I have waited so hopefully? I hear no peace in the trumpet. A shrill note and a syncopating rhythm forewarn me of a world I do not want to re-enter. And now, looking at you, awakener of the twentieth century, mouthpiece of the trumpet, I hesitate to open my lips again to start that fight which I won once, but which I cannot repeat, because my life does not flow that way anymore. I shudder and shake, seeing your bizarre clothing, your clownlike garb with long trousers and narrow fitting tunic. Who are you? Why confront me with your age of the future? I don't belong among your kind. I hear abominable noises of snorting and clanking metals around you. Leave – leave me, apparition, so that I can stay in my heavenly rest, in the realm of my peace-loving Christ, where the birds mingled their voices with the angelic, and the rustling feathers of divine wings beat the rhythmic drums of the Heavenly Choirs."

I answer: "Wilfrid, I hear your voice, and the agony in it which came with my presence. The echo of Gabriel's trumpet is with me, I know; that is my lot and my destiny. Forgive me if I disturb your heavenly rest, but I can be heard only by that part of your soul which lies listening, listening. Do you hear me? For centuries now, it has lain listening for the very sound you dislike, love, and long for. With me lies the redemption of all that could not be comprehended in your age, that looked-for, long-awaited power of the new enlightenment. Oh, I love you, Wilfrid, and all you did in your deeply moving life. In God's Hands rests the constantly rotating force of change, and with that the supreme opportunity for greater consciousness. All that could not be lived out, and was, and is still in your soul lies listening and does not come to rest until it has found its own world.

"You were never dead. You were slumbering and waiting for your Redeemer, and now you hear the trumpet of Gabriel the messenger. You hear him because your time of redemption is at hand. Not that you sinned so much, no indeed, but in living fully what you were meant to live, you have a spot of not-knowing, a dark field in the brilliance of your life achievement. All that we are, and all that we are not, both have a place. All achievement is limited by its very creation, and all creation of any kind has a shadow side. That shadow side that, not-knowing, is our teacher, and that teacher of the dark unknown is our Redeemer."

"Go away, you rascal! I know what I did better than you! I know the world well, and you can't tell me that the prisons and dungeons have disappeared. The greed, the narrowness, the jealousies of my century, I am sure, are flowering abundantly in your new age. Go away! And take that part which you say only slumbers. Go, I say!

"No, no, no, don't go! There is a pain in my heart, a spasm, a cramp which belies my peaceful state. This pain, just now, penetrates me. What is happening? A deep uneasiness, I sense. I thought I had put it to sleep at my death. The church choirs drowned my unresolved uneasiness, which I now feel again. Erlo, I must speak, listen! Now, after all these years, I sense a strange phenomenon, a new awareness. They said that I was awkward, that I was brusque and too forceful. Accused I am of not listening to my contemporaries and brusquely overriding them with my own and mostly better opinions. These primitive country bumpkins trying to deal with matters of the Church were often an abomination to me. But, curiously enough, I sense an uneasiness. Could it be that I was unwilling to understand such primitive mentality or ignorance? And haughtily went ahead?"

I answer: "What makes you say this now? Is that the story of your heart? Is that the sudden pain of a hidden truth which could not surface until now?"

"What do you want from me, Erlo? I don't like what you say. I feel pained. It is an uncomfortable awakening, another field, another world far from my blissful state of..."

"Ignoring a truth," I bluntly interrupt. Wilfrid looks at me with his grey-green eyes. His well-shaped mouth and his long, inquisitive nose, in fact all his features, are now sharply brought out; not a part of him is left out of focus to my eyes. He stands proudly, defiantly, stamping his staff. My God, I think, what a dear child of God, what a spoiled youngster he is.

Wilfrid is furious. He raises his crosier, which turns suddenly into a huge, long trumpet. It emits a groan that intensifies into the clearest penetrating note, shattering forever Wilfrid's sleep of innocence and ignorance. Shuddering as if in a fever, he hands me the symbol of his shepherd's role which has become the awakener of his soul: "Take this from me, it has turned against me. I am no longer the one I was and made of myself. Peace has fled from me and doubt is my companion."

His quick mind suddenly turns on me:

"Erlo, what made you come?"

"Aquarius, I suppose."

"Who is he?"

"The new shepherd who will unite the unknown with the known. From where that came out of me, I don't know, but nothing in me wants to change it."

"Where does he come from?"

"Out of me, and the pain of your heart, Wilfrid."

Wilfrid listens intently, then asks: "Is he – is he – a man of sorrow?"

"That is how he announced himself to you, and that is how he entered your consciousness."

"Pain, pain, oh God, deliver me from more pain." He puts his left hand on his heart and it slowly travels down his spleen to his hips where it rests. "Pain, pain, I must be back on earth again, pulled into another focus, another awareness of my heart. Oh, sweet Jesus, have mercy, have mercy, for in this land of the earth in which we are all sinners, I don't want to live any more. In the name of the Trinity and all that is Holy, don't let me return to earth without a greater Light, a greater help! Neither do I want to live a repeat, another fight for the glory of God, another campaign against the slothful man, the sluts, the slander, the pathetic ignorance of jealousy, the intolerance – none of that.

I refuse, I rebel, I won't, I can't! Back to my haven, back to my rest, back to oblivion if need be, but not any more what was. Oh God, no more of what was!"

I listen to the desperate saint of the past, and not a word of comfort escapes my lips. Nothing comes to my help. The despair is too complete, too overwhelming. I must respect this deep suffering. Curiously enough, it seems to ennoble my heart. What a dichotomy! Such stark suffering should not be made cheap by my comfort. It is so true that it will find its own way in God's spirit, and thus it will create its own answer.

Wilfrid turns away and thinks of all his travail. A powerful wave of memory engulfs him. He looks at the roots of his personality with the questioning mind of an Aquarian.

"Was my work for nothing? Did I start all these monasteries out of vanity? Was I so wrong in doing away with the Pagan mysteries?"

"No, no," I answer, "it all had to be done then, but this is another time."

"My congregation, my flock, they still pray for me," says Wilfrid, "I hear them. I can even hear the bells in the church towers. They still call the people to prayer and they still implore me to be the bridge to Christ. And I still answer their calls. Am I to shut them out and ignore them?"

"No, Wilfrid, answer their calls, but don't continue to hold humanity to the orthodox forms any longer. Support their real needs, but don't restrict your followers to the old rules. The New Ways have more freedom and include the Dark as well as the Light. Evil is not to be despised, but suffered and understood.

"Oh, dear Wilfrid, thank you. Thank you for all the good works you have done and for the things done in your name. Visit the churches and tell them about the new tidings of tolerance. Tell them that Christ has His shadow, or Dark Brother, and that the Dark Brother, Judas Iscariot, is God's being also. The new consciousness can come only through that recognition."

Wilfrid does not want to hear this.

"Will they stop praying for me?"

"Do you mean praying for you or to you?"

"As they prayed, I was so proud and felt holy."

"Wilfrid, you rascal, there lies your vanity. The aeon is over. Your holiness must come to its end, as you ended the life of the pagan Gods. But, like them, you can live in golden memory if you accept the Shadow of God, of Christ, of Jesus, and so allow the new to enter as you did before."

"I know," Wilfrid answers, "I know. The Shadow of Christ is very hard for me to accept. I have helped to fight it for so long. I know I am fighting the acceptance of all the shadow part of life. But do I have to say good-bye to "my Christ," to that world of infinite beauty and spirituality? It is as if I see nothing but blackness ahead of me, but I know I can face it when I stay connected with the Light of Christ. And the Mass – it was so beautiful. I did all I could to enlarge it and glorify it. Do I say good-bye to that too?"

"Yes, to its form, but not to its magic, nor to Christ, for that great spirit should never be denied. Be all-inclusive and welcome Light and Darkness, each in turn as they come. But judge both! In that lies your power now, and your gift to God."

"I will try, but centuries of custom are not easily set aside."

"If you don't follow the New, dear Wilfrid, there is an inevitable curse on you for preventing the living spirit of Aquarius from coming through. Now let us pray and meditate and say farewell to your beloved churches as you remember them. But please, oh please, relinquish your vanities, your personal longings, and all that stands between you and the spirit of Christ with his Dark Brother."

While praying, we are transported imperceptibly to Ripon, Wilfrid's favorite church in Yorkshire. On the altar, I plant a wooden black cross, upside down, next to the cross already there. Wilfrid, remembering his great fights for the rights of Rome, at first feels devastated that he has to listen to another authority, which is not from the Pope or the Church, but from a human being. He looks at me and, while our eyes meet, his heart starts to beat wildly, because, deep in his bowels, it rumbles. "The authority lies within you and not outside in a church. Stay true to your nature, kiss the altar, say good-bye and be a trailblazer. You are and were born that way."

Slowly, Wilfrid accepts the inevitable. He knows his inner voices. He turns around and embraces the columns of his church. It is as if, with his newly acquired wisdom, he were pulling down its ancient structure. Then, with a shudder, he seems to shake off the past. I quickly take Wilfrid by the arm and talk animatedly about the changes of the time, for, suddenly, I cannot bear the idea of that ancient holy place being undone by our modern thoughts. I do not know who is more afraid. Wilfrid seems less disturbed than I. His trail-blazing spirit is still with him, apparently, and at this moment I am more fearful than he is about the undoing of the past.

My incessant, almost forced conversation keeps Wilfrid occupied on our way to Harrowgate, where we enter the modern church built in his honor and say our prayers at its altar. Here, Wilfrid is deeply moved. He gropes for his new roots and asks for the acceptance of Christ and His Shadow and the recognition of the new Light. Listening in bewilderment are the spirits of the past and present. Is this their Saint Wilfrid, they wonder? He begs his spirit congregation to help him and thus themselves. Moving slowly through the multitude which is gathering around him, he murmurs: "Pray for your soul, pray for your soul and remember the dark night which brought redemption. Remember the crucifixion with its glorious resurrection. Don't deny the darkness its power which the Christ turned into God's light." Thus, speaking as if in a trance, he leaves the church.

At the side portal, he looks back and makes the sign of the cross over his congregation. As always, Wilfrid is looking for solutions in the very center of authority. He grasps the fact that it is now not Rome but the city of God which must provide. So he addresses his followers.

"I am on my way, on my pilgrimage to the seat of my own soul, Jerusalem, the City of God, and advise you, my beloved congregation, to do the same." At that very moment, a Light emerges in the church and lights up the spirit of all those around. As each takes a part of that Light for guidance in search of his own soul, they file out in deepest silence. The church becomes an empty shell.

Sadly, we leave them to continue our journey to the mighty Minister of York, the seat of Wilfrid's archbishopric. As

Primate of England, he is made welcome by one of his successors, the powerful Walter de Gray, thrice Regent of England. The tall, majestic archbishop rises out of his sleep wearing the splendorous robes in which he was laid to rest. On his hand glitters the enormous ring with emeralds clutching an opal. The golden lions on his silk bandolier show clearly as he opens his arms wide to embrace his ancestor. As he does so, he awakens from his trance-like state and becomes aware simultaneously of Wilfrid's bewildering journey from Ripon. At the same time, the plan for the pilgrimage to Jerusalem is revealed to him.

The proud bishop senses a new wavelength. Oh, how he hates unknown forces. They can only be wicked, and his own blackness, so well concealed during his lifetime, jumps to the fore.

"Out!" he roars at me, imperiously pointing to the doors. "Out, you blasphemer, undoer of Christ's will!"

A peal of laughter escapes my throat. I also roar, but with laughter. Wilfrid is baffled at how I handle this hostility.

"Out!" shouts Walter again, less loud and imperiously. But nothing in me moves.

"Walter," I say, "calm down. Come down from your throne and remember the times when your ill-placed authority didn't call on Christ's will. Follow Wilfrid's example and listen to your inner authority. Give up your fears and stay with your deathbed resolutions. You asked for understanding and compassion. Try to be as humble as you were then. Don't let your fear of my new authority bring you back to your weakness."

Walter looks at me with incredulity. He is so taken aback that he does not realize that, during our spat, a chain has mysteriously appeared, linking the wrists of Walter and Wilfrid. It is a light chain made of wrought iron, and I am subsequently joined in the same way to them. Like three holy pilgrims of unavoidable doom, we move now toward the main altar, to pray, to say good-bye.

I feel Walter pulling at his chain so hard that it hurts my wrist. Suddenly, he yanks sharply and stands still. "Not so fast, stranger," he says to me. "I will not undo so soon what I built up. Little do you know how hard I fought to achieve my worldly wealth. I enriched this church with priceless treasures. I built the church of Ripon almost anew. Thrice I ruled the land for the King. It took all my cunning and strength to establish my bishopric on a permanent basis so that no King with greedy hands could interfere in our church properties. No tampering now with my church. No debacles, no doom. The old spirit suffices for me."

There he stands, champing at the bit, that extremely tall man, almost six feet four, a magnetic personality, with unusual brown eyes and flaring nostrils. What a figure! This time, I don't laugh, fully realizing the shock of the awakening and the seriousness of my visit with its devastating powers.

"Come along, Walter, you and I, as well as Wilfrid, are in the grip of the unalterable spirit of the New Times." I feel for him, and it is in my voice. Slowly, I start to walk again. "What awoke you, Walter?" I ask.

"Don't ask, don't ask, I don't want to recall my waking dream. It was frightening, and those trumpets, those trumpets!"

Now, there is silence; only our shuffling feet are heard on the stones of the vast edifice. But Walter has to speak, he has to share with us; it is too much for him to carry the awakening by himself.

Agitatedly, he begins again: "That haunted dream vision! While still half asleep, I saw wildly galloping horses coming across the green hills, men and women mounted, some blind, some naked, fiercely swinging their arms. Hair flying, like furies they came. Then they suddenly halted in front of a crucifix beside a narrow path, overshadowed by an ancient tree – oh, no, don't," Walter moans, tears rolling down his cheeks. But he has to continue: "They tore ... they tore the Christ from the cross. Their hands were bleeding. It was as if each were wearing His thorny crown, and blood streamed down their faces. Oh, God! They prayed and shouted: "Lord, descend into us. The earth is parched, only our feet can make the soil fertile again, when we are imbued by you." At that, the earth flamed up as if the spirits of the underworld had risen. And there was a union of man, spirit and earth, and my bowels groaned.

"Oh God, have mercy, oh Lord, have mercy. Mary, Mary, Mother of Christ, bestow your wonders on my being."

Walter leans against a pew. His hand moves across the wooden curves as though he could wring help out of that wood.

Wilfrid and I look at each other, perplexed and moved, for here is another story of the coming of the New Age, with all its wild untamed forces, a cry from the hidden soul, coming over the horizon like a sun throwing its first light in search of salvation.

I don't talk; I sigh and my eyes brim over. Wilfrid heaves a sob and says: "Come on, Walter, you have told us the way. The flame of earth has to meet the Christ, and the bloodbath is as unavoidable as the pilgrimage to our salvation." Walter looks at us. He cannot yet comprehend all, but, relieved by his communing, he follows, disarmed. No fight is left in him. Slowly, we proceed, laden with the bitter reality of the awakening dream-vision.

The stones again echoing our steps, Walter, touching each pew as we proceed, begins anew: "Wilfrid," he says, "I want to talk with you. I feel, when I speak to you, that I am speaking to a father, perhaps to the great ancestor." He smiles. "I am not sure I know Him, but He must be in my blood and I feel I can touch him if I tell you about my life. Perhaps then I will know more about the purpose of my travail."

We stand now in front of the altar steps, and it comes to me that the thirteenth century did not speak much, if at all, about the Ancestor. I can't help smiling as it becomes obvious that another spirit is already entering into Walter.

While observing this, we mount the steps. Three chairs miraculously appear and we seat ourselves in them. I look at the altar and notice that a shadowy outline of a figure is leaning against the ancient sacrificial stone, partly hiding the cross from me. Then I hear Walter's voice again: "Wilfrid, you must know that I built a shrine for you. I remember so well holding your skull in my hands, thinking of you, and feeling you even in my bones. When I put it to rest, it made me think of an apple fallen from a tree. I admired your life and its tenacity. I prayed to you, for you – not knowing you are part of me. That knowledge rises up now, as if it were an old truth, and it gives me an inner peace."

He pauses a while, cherishing that new, wonderful truth. Smilingly, he continues: "I worked well and I lived well. I enriched my family and my church, and I was the Church. Many times did I travel as ambassador for good King John." The "good" surprises him and makes him smile. "I was three times Regent of England for his son, King Henry, who knew I was a good organizer and could squeeze out provisions for his army in France. I loved the boy, but did not like him, always.

"Born ambitious, the hard blows of life made me cunning. I have been called avaricious; perhaps it is true but I don't feel it that way. I can be tough, but, now, telling this, I realize that I had to learn to wield power, to taste it, to become aware of what that power does to others and, above all, what that power does or did to me. Frankly, you can never become detached from this world or evaluate it properly until you have experienced its riches. That haughty, priestly attitude of phony simplicity has no value when it is just withdrawal from life. I can't see the magic in that. I lived richly and loved it. Not until I was older did I comprehend the meaning of simplicity; only then could my ambitious side taste other realities. My true spirit entered on my death; it was pure joy and put the struggles of my earth life in perspective. In the annals, they say that, at the end, I was weak in my brains. I was not; never was I clearer. First I suffered deeply, agonizingly, as I spoke to my soul. The earth had taken my spirit, and then given it back. I became free and my spirit soared. I died happily and peacefully. You have no idea of the relief, the immense relief. My task was done.

"Your life, your times were so different, Wilfrid. I am a child of the Magna Carta. When I rode out with King John from Windsor, little did I suspect that I would spend the last days of my life in parliament trying to teach the nobles the rules of that game. There was no more cunning or greed left in me. Service became natural, but what a long road I had had to travel! In my soul, Wilfrid, there must have been a memory of your troubles with rough kings. John most unroyally sold my estates while I was his ambassador to France. He needed the money to pay the Pope for my bishop's seat in York. When I came back, I was York, surrounded by much glory and pomp; the King had more power in the church and I was as poor as Job." Walter smiles almost maliciously. "But not for long. Whatever they say about me, I did not impoverish my flock, the estates were well taken care of. Of course, my family got richer, but those were hard times.

"When John died, Henry was crowned and I anointed him, well do I remember. My privileged position to the crown tipped the scales. Greed and power took control. I trusted neither man nor beast. It was as if I had taken root in the cunning of the times. I loathed the regents of Henry III. I wanted to outsmart them, but in my way. The occult always had great interest for me, and so I decided..."

But Walter could not continue. Then, after a while, he spoke again. "I was, I am an archbishop. That means the apostolic blessing is carried by me. It is the greatest treasure given to me, perhaps the only true jewel there is, and now... Oh, my God, I feel low, very low." He slumps in his chair, his knees seek the ground and he drops to the altar floor, a crumpled figure. After a while, he calmly and almost majestically gets up. Standing straight, he speaks without a trace of pity for himself. "You know, Wilfrid, I confessed this once; but now you are here and, on my right, this new version of our spirit with his trumpeteer, and so I have to repeat my confession to the past and the future.

"My very darkest nature forced me even to say the black mass in order to get power over the young King. Thank God,

I failed. I suppose that the blessings of Him whom I carry counteracted my poisonous self. Thrice did I say that mass; it haunted me and, in the end, purified my existence. I have lived it out painfully. But my inner being suffers it still.

"Telling this makes me understand more about my vision of this morning: the incoherent darkness of the soul has to be redeemed. The time has come for another Darkness, but black it is. The ignorance of evil is still its tool. I know that power in me and I accept it. God grant me strength to suffer it into awareness, wherever I am." At that, two large tears of blood drop on the altar.

Walter sees them. He turns towards me: "Let us proceed, Erlo. I knew your name but could not bear pronouncing it before. Let us proceed and accept the times which have awakened me. My incomplete self, my questing soul I will follow throughout the ages. I know about my immortality and I never lived it. Now I do."

We proceed to the altar and kneel in prayer. Next to the golden cross standing in the middle, I install a second one of black corroded silver. It makes Walter shiver. He holds on to Wilfrid, and the three of us start on our way to the south transept, where we entered. It is as if I have to pull those two powerful bishops along.

Suddenly, a clatter. The chains are broken. I turn around and see Walter and Wilfrid disappear into one of the enormous columns. I stand unshackled and alone in the huge cathedral. The Stones of the column then speak with their voices. First a whisper, then a thundering voice declares: "We are the Church; we stay here. We are the Light; we shun the Shadow."

A black-winged thought of the Preserver, that powerful Lord of cosmic order, has gripped the soul of my companions. That unyielding aspect of God has taken hold of my friends. In that stifling moment, creation or destruction come to naught. All is as ever and forever. It is a truly holy attempt to preserve what is, a counteraction to all the shocking events – a self-preservation which will not work, though we try and have a powerful ally. But we cannot change the moment or stop the natural flow of the new breath of life.

But I too am stifled. I try to remain with the known: this also is instinctive. The fear of the unknown in me is so great, I know it so well. I pray to the Lord Preserver to bestow on us the memories of the past in an indelible way so that nothing be lost of our journeys on earth or even in heaven. I pay my tribute to that benign power which also gives us the mercy of rest so that we may continue. I reach out to the stones in the column. I stroke them and feel with my ancient friends the shock we have had. First, I think there is nothing for me to do but go my way. But how can I, without them?

As I stand irresolute, I see that, slowly, the stones take on form again. The two men stand before me. Reluctantly, they emerge from the column, kneel before me and say: “We want to stay.” They are like two youths, contrite and unwilling to mature. I want both of them with me and I cannot leave them behind. They embrace each other and, once again, disappear into the stones, but this time through the floor. Then they arise in back of me, tears streaming down their cheeks. I feel as if they are now in my aura, like a psychic backbone. Together, we ceremoniously kiss the floor, the walls and wave to the altar.

Slowly leaving the cathedral, we are accompanied by a host of angels and the sound of great music from the organ and chorus singing a last Te Deum. Then, as Walter and Wilfrid precede me, the spirits of the past and present gather about us, bow, kneel and wave tearful good-byes. Their tears are for the departing saints and leaders of their church. Now they stand painfully on their own. I feel that they, too, will go on their lone pilgrimage. In the large doorway of the transept Walter had built, we turn around and, with both doors open wide, we kneel to pray for the future of the Church – if there is to be such a thing. Suddenly two – no, one little devil appears out of the ground, a remnant spirit from the crypt. He kisses Walter and embraces Wilfrid. He is to stay behind.

But now, from nowhere, Kerel appears, the mighty Kyros, personification of all that man has experienced since time immemorial. He is truly a breathtaking figure – fully six feet tall, with a lionesque head, a wide forehead, piercing eyes which cannot hide the suffering of mankind, and a generous mouth. He stands in utter self-composure. Pointing at the little devil, he says: "Take that little fellow with you. The break has to be complete and forever." At that fierce command, the huge cathedral cracks and crumbles. The thunderous rumble is bone-chilling. It is the end. It is God's command, the spirit of the times functioning through the presence of those who are called upon.

I sway from the impact of this debacle; still, I feel slightly comforted by the nearness of Kerel. The great bishops, however, move away in utter horror. I look back sadly on the column of dust which rises slowly heavenward from the rubble. Wilfrid and Walter cannot. They stare ahead, hopelessly shaken by what has happened. I see Kerel entering the chaos of stone pillars, broken walls and windows. Then, in the middle of that havoc, he stretches his arms heavenward in supplication. I hear him ask: "Lord, will there be an answer to this?"

Our pilgrim's path now leads toward that difficult stumbling block of their ambitions, Canterbury, the mighty fortress of English spirituality. Wilfrid does not even like the mention of that name because it brings back so many controversies, so much unhappiness. Thank God there was a Rome to rule over it, he thinks.

Walter smiles grimly. Canterbury never allowed him to annex Scotland. He would have loved the title of Primate of England and Scotland, almost more imposing than Canterbury's title of Primate of all England. His eyebrows rise for a moment at the thought of all that vanity. "Who knows, it is still in me," he sighs. I look contentedly at my companions. We are now on horseback, the ancient knightly way of traveling.

The town of York disappears behind the horizon. We go farther and farther through the medieval woods and green pastures of this emerald island. Something makes me look back. The column of smoke of York's cathedral is now a dark cloud traveling with us like a shadow companion.

We have been a long time in the saddle. Apparently, our psyches are not so very anxious to proceed. I notice that our horses are trotting slowly. Then they start to walk almost lazily. We make no attempt to hurry them on. Now we go through a meadow path, over the hill, and there it lies, Canterbury with its magnificent towers and spires. I take a deep breath of the clear air and sigh. The horses sense our uneasiness and apprehension, and seem reluctant to carry us any farther. We dismount on a grassy slope outside the town as if, in that way, we could protect God's house of stone from any debacle.

There is no chapel or wayside station, so we kneel on the grass. God's creation is our church. The heaven above is spotlessly blue and the earth's incense is the fragrance of the wildflowers. It is the Creator's earth and heaven, and ours. We pray for the union of earth and heaven so that a marriage may take place in our souls that will unite the Darkness of the earth with the Heavenly Light. We pray for another marriage of Adam and Eve, but, this time, with the blessing of the Creator. Deeper we go into prayer. I sense the stillness of soul in my two bishop brothers; it penetrates my heart and puts it in a deep rest. I sigh and sigh again as peace descends into my being. At that moment, we hear a fearful rumbling in the earth as it heaves with a terrifying sigh, like a panting breast. The heart of God seems to beat faster inside his immense earth body. Cracks appear in the land and thunder is heard. A faint smell starts to emanate from beneath us and, as we continue to pray in deepest fear of the Lord, we see from afar the toppling walls of mighty Canterbury. The roof falls, towers sway, windows break and a huge rocket of fire rises heavenward, bursts, and disperses itself in a sickening stench. The cathedral crumbles; tiny pieces of black grit fall at our feet – souvenirs for the pilgrims of the future.

Stunned by the devastation and awed by the might of the

new powers around us, Walter, Wilfrid, and I leave and travel on to the Channel. They both know that, when they make the crossing, there will be no return to their England. Both of these men have ruled the land as kingly priests; they look back to say farewell to their former domains, but even more to say farewell to their deeply loved country, to which they have given their lives. They are true patriots with profound compassion for their homeland.

Aroused from his sleep, François de Salignac de la Mothe-Fénelon, Archbishop of Cambrai, tutor to the Duke of Bourgogne, author, philosopher, educator, religious advisor to the court of Louis XIV – and an exile in Cambrai – is awaiting the wayfaring bishops, his English ancestors. His noble French seventeenth century mind is wondering what will happen.

All his full and distinguished life, he carried the sweet, gentle beauty of the Dordogne in his heart. That gentleness is of his essence and is his strength; with that, he faced his exile and the rebukes of his enemies. And with the same fortitude and sweetness of soul, he now awaits the arrival of Wilfrid and Walter. The spirit of the times has made him aware, by its unseen power, that his existence is not yet over. Something unfulfilled needs completion. The dawning consciousness of the age of enlightenment, of which he is so proud, is not enough for the time at hand.

Rubbing his eyes and shaking his head, he tries to understand the message but feels only apprehension and bewilderment as he hears and even vaguely sees – like a moving panorama – the events which happened to his brethren. He sees the upside-down cross and the black one. Like a flash, it occurs to him that Peter was crucified that way; well might that ancient, strange symbol be emphasized. But, as usual, he tries to reason and understand with only that part of his heart which readily accepts all gentlemanly understanding and abhors and shuts out all vulgarity of spirit. The dignity of the Catholic church is the measure of his heart.

As he moves to the south portal of his cathedral to welcome his visitors, he experiences a vision of Wilfrid and Walter – just their four eyes, with four or five tears of blood. They seem to express a depth of suffering he has never experienced himself. He quickly returns to his sanctuary, aware that this vision is not just a fantasy, but a deadly truth which is about to hit him. Neither the cultured façade of his seventeenth century nor his rigorous obedience to Rome's rule, which had so penetrated his being, would suffice to meet the power about to confront him. These attitudes of the past would act as poison to the unity of Light and Shadow.

Fénelon rushes to his bishop's throne and seats himself. Dressed in simple priestly robes, he anxiously awaits Walter and Wilfrid's arrival. The moment of revelation is upon him. The end of his world is near, a world which is more complicated and rational, less primitive than theirs. But François possesses the capacity for true suffering which has always enhanced his world with a beauty and sensitivity rare for a man of such culture and elegance. He deals with life in utter spiritual refinement. But these orientations alone are not enough to support life as it is lived now. His bulwark is the love of his people: "*Mais le peuple m'adore,*" he thinks. Somewhere he is still vain, and he knows it.

Somehow, I cannot talk with François. He is so close to me that a dialogue cannot take place. My vision, my fantasy are his. We are like one, and I am sucked into an area of my psyche where I am powerless. I must identify with this bishop of the early eighteenth century. I suffer with him; my duality of consciousness has ceased to be. I am like Fénelon. I AM – oh my God – Fénelon. There is no separation. I was he and I am he. He is alive in me – what a thing to accept. I might as well write "I" instead of François. Still, I am Erlo – and also François.

François turns his head towards the altar so that he will avoid witnessing the magical entrance of his ancestors, powerful men in the affairs of Church and state. They have gone through the whole debacle of their churches, and now his turn has come. Not only does he sense it, he knows it. He does not dare to turn around, but he realizes that the doors of the cathedral are open. He stands up and goes to the altar in order to keep his back toward the pilgrims, and to pray for the last time to the single Christ, His Glory, His Light. There is no Shadow, only Light, His Light.

Now, in his most beautiful robes, but with the heart of a simple priest, Fénelon prays, hoping perhaps to forestall his fate. "Good-bye, Lord Christ, Glory of Light, only begotten Son of the Most High!" There is no music. The organ is silent, no cry is heard except that of the lost priest. It is his last devout, truly holy attempt to call on God's son, Jesus: "Have mercy, oh Lord, pity my heart, where Jesus Christ founded my home. Do not destroy my Light, which gave me the strength to carry my life with fortitude. Spare my cathedral – my church, the mother of my congregation, and don't, I pray, disrobe my soul of its garment. What else can protect me from the rigors of life? In my weakness, I need your help for survival. Only begotten one of the Most High, I beg you, listen to this supplicant. Don't leave me, oh Lord Jesus, have mercy, Lord have mercy!"

François resembles a man taken from the cross with bleeding wounds and a lost soul. Then a vision comes to life, he sees his Christ dethroned, an emptied cross, – no cross. And then, oh God, it happens. The altar bursts open. From it a black cloud rises, and out of stark darkness two men emerge – one all Light and one all Dark. They embrace, entwine and clasp hands to signify the new powers rising out of the ancient altar. Now Darkness and Light are one and indivisible. The New Age is here. Christianity is dead.

I burst into tears, can't write a word. This death is too much to take. What will happen? Centuries of unsolved life are upon me. My support is gone; I stand alone. Now I look at François in a different way. I see him devastated but within me.

There is, however, in me a core, educated differently, already immersed in another spirit so I am set free from my beloved Fénelon. My tears dissolve the total identification and, gradually, I come to the place where I can write again. Now the scene in the church opens up clearly before my mind's eye.

Wilfrid and Walter, who have traversed the long apse of the church while François was praying, put their arms around his waist. There they stand, taking in the awesome apparition, Walter on the left, François in the middle and Wilfrid, shadowy from agony and fear, on his right. They kneel with bowed heads knowing this is the revelation they seek; this is the New Moment, the life to come. No music. No organ. Only the dead silence of the awful birth. Then a howling note of cosmic agony booms through the church. All becomes more vibrant.

François shudders; he can't bear the sight of this new image of God. He turns around and so witnesses his debacle. The church walls dissolve into a column of dust. The cathedral is dust. Wilfrid and Walter see only the apparition, the entwined brothers of Darkness and Light, the new symbol of power and wholeness. François slowly turns again, trying to accept the new Light, this altar-born vision of what-is-and-always-was, even before Christ. Gradually the connection with his rational mind is coming back. It occurs to him that the idea of the vision, while shocking and disturbing, is otherwise quite logical and clear.

At that moment, Kerel appears again, because François attempts to intellectualize the true meaning of the vision instead of emotionally reacting to its power. This rationalist attitude would dry up the forces of the living spirit. "To hell with your spirit-killing intellect!" Kerel shouts, and with a powerful sweep of his arm, the last root of François' rational attitude is pulled out and laid to dry on the debris of the church floor.

François shivers as if a wind were blowing through him and stripping him of his clothing. Sobbing, he falls to the floor as the new spirit of the vision enters him. Wilfrid and Walter come to his help and, as they lift him to his feet, the three experience a quickening and deepening of the understanding and powers of the mighty new Holy Ghost.

In a flash of recognition, François becomes aware of a new disposition, another attitude towards life. His long career of educating the royal princes, the noble ladies – the sophisticated snobs of the intelligentsia – passes through his head. He becomes painfully conscious of the one-sidedness of his beloved Church. He recalls his sermons and his letters, always emphasizing nobleness of thought and action while turning a half-deaf ear and a blind stare to the importance of all that and those lost in the darkness of the devil's grip. "Oh God, will I ever embrace that darkness with enough love and compassion for its redemption? How much I have to learn and understand!" He crosses himself in the name of the Father and the Son and the Holy Ghost, and adds slowly "and the Holy Mother." No more Trinity alone; the power of the earth has to be included.

Kerel, deeply satisfied with this change, stands in the midst of the crumbled church surrounded by rubble and dust. He is the pillar of the past, and the clearing house of life and death for the development of the Self. There is no music, and he can almost hear the silent passing of time. All that is orthodox in the archbishops, all the inevitable limitations of their times are vanishing. The three, in total exhaustion, accept their fate and, in so doing, unite in consciousness with Kerel. Through this union, the greater clarity of Kerel becomes part of them. His wisdom will now be available to their soul.

The Man of Light and the Man of Darkness, still clasping hands, turn toward Kerel as they descend from the altar, thus setting foot on earth for the first time. What they touch is the dust, the *prima materia* out of which their future church will have to be built.

Kerel genuflexes reverently to the newborn spirit, turns, and looks at the holocaust. Intensely moved, he picks his way through the aperture where once the great doors gave entrance to the church. The wide open landscape in front of him, the flatlands of Northern France, shows nothing but endless bleakness. Far in the distance is their next beacon on this devastating but holy pilgrimage, Rome. Kerel leads the way, followed by François, Walter, Wilfrid, then me, and, behind us, the two Sons of God, the two Christs next to each other, clasping hands.

It is a great moment in time. What will happen to Rome, the seat of supreme authority, where the throne of Saint Peter has been occupied for centuries by his successors? What will our presence do to that glorious city?

August 9, 1966
Sils Maria

And so I watch with my inner eye. There they go, first Kerel, then François and Walter next to each other and, falling behind, Wilfrid, the least willing and the most sad. He almost disappears in a mist, but he has to go along. He experienced the Christ in the first millennium and overcame evil so many times in his life that to accept the Dark Son of God still seems sheer folly to him. "Oh God," Wilfrid sighs, "couldn't I have stayed asleep, untouched by time? Your power, Your kingdom, oh Lord, is more than weird. Now to know that Darkness and Light are expressions of one nature is too overwhelming. Both Your Will and Glory make me fear You all the more."

Wilfrid looks back and sees again the dual figures of the two Sons of God – only now they are surrounded by a glow of soft light. This image is to follow and become part of them, as inseparable as a cloud is to rain. In this manner, they travel on.

I see them now, crossing the land of François, beautiful France. It is his country. So many of his ancestral family fought here, and had their glories, defeats and capers. François is France, as Wilfrid and Walter are England. François is well aware of the many, many connections which bind him to this country. The Gramont, the Montmorency, the Salignac, the de la Motte-Houdancourt, the Bourbon, and many more soul connections slumber in his heart. During this pilgrimage, he integrates the mane of these many lives lived with such intensity. All this rises up in François' mind and strengthens his backbone. Then another powerful wave of memories comes over him. He recalls the papal authority; he thinks of his defeat in Rome and the Pope's fear of Louis XIV. He remembers that, in a way, he wanted to be a cardinal; he knows he deserved the honor. He does not condemn the Pope, but feels a great sadness about the whole miserable Bossuet affair, his defeat by that powerful Bishop of Meaux. He is almost morose for a moment as he recalls that the powers of the spirit could be vanquished by ignorance, fear and anxiety. Rome was simply unable to accept the truth. Power won. Evil held court. "I bowed my head reverently," he remembers, "in obedience to the spirit of the Church, the survival of Christ's Church, not because I feared the Pope." Ignorance made its force felt and darkness ruled Rome. The royal crown had become shabby. François is back again in olden times with his unsolved problems. He shakes himself out of his reverie and thinks: "That must now be over. Now my prayers, my devout prayers must be for the life of the soul with its new vision – not only for the Christ as I knew him. But can the Dark Brother bring redemption? Will I dare to speak the whole truth in the coming age without being punished by some vengeful authority?"

Kerel has observed François and registers his thoughts. Now he turns to him: "François, anything which does away with your roots is severing and would destroy the value of your experiences. Your 'friend,' Monsieur the Bishop of Meaux, whose bitter animosity tested you to the very core, and whose insidious ways almost succeeded in destroying you, was the very man you needed in order to reach the depths of your suffering and understanding."

Now Kerel, with his enigmatic smile, continues: "Did it ever occur to you, François, that the dark side of your soul can enter into a life which, knowing your foibles and weaknesses, will test your spirit of growth to the breaking point? That this Self-crucifixion can bring strength and rebirth? It is the way the Self tests earth existence to see if growth is still there, if the Tree of Life and Knowledge is still alive. François, you stayed alive in spirit; you did not stoop low but nobly went ahead. Bossuet's life accomplished its purpose to the full and, satisfied, the soul dropped it like an apple from a tree to let it rot away. Only the seeds will always live, to serve later on to test again the validity of life. I don't think that Bossuet will ever talk to you; he will be totally absorbed by you, François."

With a gracious bow and smile, François acknowledges Kerel's comment. He is impressed by his knowledge, but the moment of total acceptance has not yet come. So his courtly manner automatically comes to François' rescue. Nothing is settled in his mind yet, but Kerel has dropped a seed and knows that it will grow.

Nearer and nearer they come to Rome. They are all sad, infinitely sad and apprehensive – for what will happen to Rome? Now Wilfrid steps completely out of the mist and becomes clear. He loves Rome, for it is there that he found help and liberation in his lifetime. He wants to rush towards the Eternal City and touch the stones of Holy Church, but his feet refuse. He is torn apart, for Rome is not York or Canterbury; Rome is the center of the power he helped to establish in his homeland, and its rule was supreme. But the proud, eternal Center of the Apostolic succession has to meet its fate. "There is a time of glory, there is a time of sunrise, there is a time of sunset," he murmurs within himself. Now Wilfrid sees the cloud of York, Canterbury and Cambrai come closer and closer. He can't bear the sight. The relentless powers of the new Aeon are so gripping that again he tries to escape from them.

Spontaneously, a vision springs up in him of his Saint Peter's and the other churches he knew. He sees them, transparent, a ghostly memory of light and holiness – a memory of an all-prevailing universal truth, but without substance. The city becomes grey in his vision; it begins to rain. With the rain, the vision vanishes for ever. In this bewildered man of God, saint of the Holy Roman Church, only a memory of Rome's righteousness and fighting spirit remains.

François and Walter are not as perplexed as Wilfrid. They remember their disenchantment with Rome. They had expected truth and perspicacity to rule there, but, instead, they witnessed political manipulations. In spite of their priesthood, they now have a death wish for this holy city. So much evil, they feel, has been perpetrated in its sanctimonious atmosphere.

I see the three draw together, seeking protection in one another's nearness. They need one another, for at their feet lies the Holy City, the power, the glory of their Church which, they know, must meet its fate like all else in life. From their hilltop, they see the ever darkening sky gathering, leaving a strip of light on the horizon from where the setting sun is sending its last rays into the Eternal City. The windows, first reflecting like diamonds, become dull and then black holes. The stones and bricks are turning grey. "It is a town of clay," exclaims Walter. At that, the dark clouds emit their burden. The rain begins to pelt down-down-down – and down go the buildings as if the earth were absorbing its own. The Mother Church is received by the greater Mother Earth. Back again into the womb of darkness; as it was in the beginning, so it is in the end. To clay we return to be born again – but when? The Wheel of Life alone turns without end. All form shapes itself under its influence.

Kerel stoically stands watch over their psyche. François now weeps bitterly for the Rome which could not live up to his expectations. He feels the West was not able to produce enough men of noble spirit to set a lasting example for the rest of the world. Evil had to come and claim its power. Even the holy alchemy of the Church, he reflects, was not strong enough to stem the *Zeitgeist* of disintegration.

I think, unless the Dark wants to redeem itself, how can we ever live with the darkness of God's spirit?

Strong, rugged Walter, aware of François' deep religious feeling, turns to him and says: "My dear Fénelon, working with the Magna Carta, Parliament, the King and the Pope gave me a deep insight into worldly affairs. I see them as the temporary fruit of man's psychic history. I knew also that Rome could never bridge the worlds of the Crown and the Cross. In spite of this, my eyes were always on Rome. They should have been on Jerusalem, the roots of our spiritual heritage. That was my mistake."

Kerel knows full well that Rome had replaced Jerusalem. Neither François nor Wilfrid had ever realized that Walter also knew that. Wisdom comes from men who have handled the dark ways of life. The Black Mass which Walter once said to gain power over his youthful King has led him through the deepest darkness of suffering to the Light at the left hand of God.

Tighter and tighter they unite, needing one another's experience and holding on to the hope that in the blackness a degree of comprehension of the source of life can be found. Isn't that our quest?

Kerel is laden with the heavy heart of mankind as he begins to realize that the new spirit of the dual vision is, as yet, a total unknown – a cloud, a grey substance in which the light of pure spirit has disappeared.

Unwilling to enter Rome, the wayfarers travel around the city in a half circle towards the West and, in doing so, throw their shadows on Rome – once so great, so powerful, so corrupt, so worshipped. Only the light of the setting sun of a new day – mature, forgiving, full of warmth and understanding – can pay a fitting last tribute to the ruin that is Peter's Church.

Now I see them standing south of Rome: François, Walter, Wilfrid and Kerel and, further to the north, Christ and His Shadow-Brother. They know that Europe has to be left behind, but then, as one, they hesitate, they waver. Must they cross the Hellespont back to Asia? Must they leave Europe? Can't they go to Greece? Is Jerusalem so very important? Did the spirit of Greece not contribute brilliantly to the Christian mind? The West is their home, their love, and what might befall them if they cross over the waters to the cradle of Christianity? From the Middle East, their spirit had been catapulted to the wilds of a primitive Europe. They came to love Europe dearly, for it was there that they suffered their lives and built their churches – and their palaces also, although our bishops don't like this reminder of their elegant, worldly ways. They all thought they were so spiritual – except for Walter, who was fully aware of the cost of stately living and the price he paid for it. Such thoughts are the best antidote for that personal halo which Wilfrid and François still have wobbling slightly around their heads.

Kerel stands as irresolute as his companions. He knows that he will be forced to become conscious of a deeper level of his Universal Self. He is about to enter the Near East. To cross the Hellespont means that he will return to the cradle of Christianity, nearer the magic battlefield of Arjuna, where Yahweh ruled when Christ was born. That was the time when the power of the Logos faced the newly budding Eros: the majesty of creation facing the flower of Love incarnate in frail humankind. An aeon of suffering has passed. What will the future bring? Kerel feels burdened, bruised and near melancholy, for where is the light of the future?

August 10, 1966
Sils Maria

I know why they hesitate and philosophize: there is an emotional block in their psyches, something not yet experienced which belongs to their pilgrimage. When they circled Rome, following the shape of the crescent moon, they made a night's journey in which much was left undigested. The farewell to the Eternal City was too painful to bear. Fear had plugged their ears; their noses had omitted the smells. They just *saw* the debacle.

Rome had cried out to them: "Save us! Save the churches of Peter and Paul!" Why Peter and Paul? Why not in the name of Christ? Rome's grey pleading voices had lost their luster. Peter and Paul are history – only the Christ is eternal.

Now, as they look back on the city, a rain of ashes and dust descends. Once it was the hope of mankind; now it is only the agony. Kerel, touched to the core, just stands and watches. The full realization of the debacle is upon them. François weeps convulsively over the lost opportunities for greatness. Walter stands silent, numb, while tears stream down his grooved face. Wilfrid, his hands lifted, begins to hum a beloved Gregorian chant which he composed with his singer, Willibald, during their pilgrimage to the Holy City. He sings firmly now and, with that alchemy, digests the pain of destruction. With each stanza, Rome sinks deeper into his heart. It is not there, out on the bleak landscape, but safely tucked away in his chest, and deeper still is his Jerusalem. What he once experienced of Rome's beauty, spirituality and strength, and carried so happily back to Ripon and York, will not be lost; neither will the Church's efforts to recreate the Kingdom of Heaven on earth. It is all well-stored within Wilfrid, and so he is the first to turn his back on the ashes and walk ahead towards his future.

The others have to stand there for a while: they are thinking. If Rome has not provided the living truth they seek, might not Jerusalem also turn their hopes into dust? Can this earth support the Heavenly Kingdom? They look at Wilfrid, going ahead with a sturdy stride; there is even a glow, an aura around his lithe body. Kerel recalls the leading spirit that is ever a part of Wilfrid and can't suppress his amusement. That priestly rascal always barges ahead once his goal is set. The others follow, for haven't they always pursued that which is numinous? They call to him and he stops, glad to have his companions join him.

"Wait, Wilfrid, where are you going?" they ask.

"To Jerusalem, of course," he answers.

"You seem to be full of portent; purpose radiates from you."

With a majestic sweep of the arm, he motions to his spirit brothers to follow him. "Come with me to Jerusalem," he shouts, "as we still must see what It may reveal to us, or what we can accomplish there." Kerel is delighted with the new mood created by this old fighter, but he is also somewhat dubious about what still lies ahead.

Before Jerusalem can be reached, there is still one more spirit brother to be visited: Asterius, Archbishop of Amasia. The Near East is much alive in Wilfrid's memory. Amasia is remembered in his Eternal Mind, and he is strongly attracted to that city. He doesn't intuit at all, however, what gruesome initiations are in store. Neither François, nor Walter, nor Kerel, for that matter, has any idea of the immense change to come which, unknowingly, they are helping to bring about.

On they go; a pioneering spirit is affecting their blood. The unseen power behind them influences every step of the way. They cannot act differently; they are caught in the vise-like grip of the new era and moved to cross the waters toward the native land of their soul.

My emotions are in upheaval. I admire my ancestral components: their spell is on me. I feel every one of them and, at times, I am torn apart. Then, again, my apprehensions are completely overridden by an inner surge of confidence. My inner being watches my progress, and I write and write. Its voice, impossible to override, is dictating to me.

The spirit of Light and Darkness, the spirit of Christ and Satanic Lucifer which has followed them from Northern France, is slowly spreading all over the world. If they had looked back, our wayfarers, if their eyes were not directed, so full of hope, towards Amasia and Jerusalem, they would have seen what Kerel knew was happening: a world in conflagration and turmoil, a miraculous merging of the numinous and nigredo meant not to destroy the past, nor to prevent the future, but to create, with terror-striking power, of being, a world in which the mighty as well as the meek spirits will seek expression to establish the next human kingdom on this Heavenly earth.

In Amasia, on the other side of the Hellespont, Asterius, totally unaware of any change to come, is laughing, for they are all coming back home. He is a stocky, strong man, and he laughs heartily and long. He will give them a wonderful welcome, and they will hear about another Christianity which he lived. No Rome nor wicked Constantinople could ever dampen his spirit, not even after Eusebius sent persecutors to try to kill him. They left him for dead by the roadside with a broken hip. Limping and undaunted, he preached in a deep voice the apostolic message according to his innate nature and his experience of the Christ Jesus within him. For almost a hundred years, he had lived that life and, with golden tongue, declared the wonders of Christ. It was a time rampant with the evil power drives of an emerging theology. But always with him are the memories of masses of people, searching for the deep experiences and ecstasies of saintly men to lift themselves out of dark primitivity into Christ-like awareness. Indeed, he fills the fourth century church of Amasia with the greatness of his vibrant personality.

I now see our wayfarers nearing Amasia, tiny figures moving on and on. I see the momentum, the roads, and, as in real life I wonder how I can travel so far, so constantly over this globe, as if in traveling I will fulfill my quest and find an answer to the question which has changed with every milestone I have reached.

Our wayfarers now reach Amasia. With his usual passionate vitality and warmth, Asterius has prepared a wonderful welcome for his friends. Astute, worldly, yet deeply religious in the purest sense, he is like a rock of strength and confidence. He never changes; no age seems to affect him. He is still in the fourth century, undaunted as ever, and completely unaware of the cosmic Now in which his soul mates travel.

In full regalia of cloth of gold, Asterius stands alone, waiting on the steps in front of the portal to the shrine of his beloved Christ. There are no crowds, there is no music, all is blue-grey. All alone, he stands there, solemn in the full majesty of his office. The entourage to which he is so accustomed is not with him. He is imbued with the powers of the Apostolic blessing and again experiences the curious mingling of Lord and servant.

He sways slightly, shakes his head, juts out his square jaw, and looks piercingly with his dark eyes into the blue-grey of his surroundings. He pushes his long hair behind his ears and wriggles inside his stocky body. Is he asleep or dreaming? His aloneness is in such contrast to the time when he stood on the very same spot – years ago – waiting to receive the bones of Saint Phocas, the first martyr to have his remains, "the tabernacle of his holy mind," installed in the Lord's shrine. Asterius is filled with a warm glow of satisfaction: he is the one who initiated the rites for the adoration and glorification of this simple martyr. "That was then," he thinks, "but what now? Am I dreaming? Asleep or awakening from my eternal slumber? How strange, this blue-grey light."

He wants to walk but cannot. His feet seem rooted in the cathedral steps. He lifts his shorter left leg; yes, it can move. He lifts his right one; yes, it moves also. But he cannot walk.

"Travel within," says his inner voice, "travel deeper and realize how your progeny, Wilfrid, became Saint of York. Remember the agonies of your soul during those barbaric days in the West. Primitive England! It made you withdraw and go back to sleep; later, you wanted to interfere in that life and force Wilfrid to stay in Rome."

"Memories of the past, flee from me! Don't haunt me with what I couldn't accomplish. Soothe me with my achievements, the great sermons, the power I had to sway the masses to adore the Lord and see His Glory!"

"No," says the inner voice, "that is all gone and done – done well, but your soul has moved on, anxious to live and perform what could not be achieved in your century. Your fourth century, like any other time, allowed just so much and accomplished only its limited tasks. Awake and await that which you did not live. Fear not. Flash your beautiful smile and look with your dark eyes on the unfolding of your soul life. See what your Self has had to experience through the centuries. The end of time is nearing. You have to know what could not be done in your Piscean Age."

"Again a call to life?" Asterius asks himself.

"Life is unending," retorts his inner voice, "no rest ever, only change from what is and was in order to experience the everlasting variety of man's expressions."

How well he knows that voice. "No wonder," he thinks, "that, five centuries after I spoke, that very same voice was so eagerly sought after in my homilies. Who knows, perhaps that is the everlasting Presence, the Unknown Divine in my soul and mind. That voice in its greatest moment spoke through Jesus." He trembles because he has experienced its emotional power so often. Tears well up, he feels a tremor in his heart like a far-off thunder – or is it perhaps the rumbling of an earthquake? It is the moment of confrontation with the unfolding of his life work and what his Center has had to experience through the centuries.

Looking down the street leading to the cathedral square, he now observes the slow approach of his expected guests. Four tired travelers they are. There is something remarkable and strange about them. Is he truly the ancestor of these men? In Kerel, he sees the glow of the Eternal Light, Wilfrid reflects the Holy spirit of Rome, Walter is like the brown earthly riches of power, and in Fénelon Asterius sees an elegance of bearing and culture that are so close to him. He notices that the stars of each of his further incarnations are shining over their heads through the dark shadows and strange lights of their auras. These are not just men – they are peculiar saints, or men imbued by a new Light unknown to him. Apprehensive now, he steps back towards the portal of his stronghold. Suddenly the building is filled with thunderous music, and he hears drums beating in strange rhythms, shrill piping, and a heavenly choir of voices singing unknown stanzas. The darkness around the heavenly aura of the four pilgrims becomes more intense now, and fierce lightning pierces the heavens. It seems as if they may be struck at any moment, but this possibility does not even occur to them.

This greatly anticipated welcome, this high moment of encounter and reunion becomes a frightening, terror-striking event to Asterius. He throws up his arms to the heavens, only to hear derisive laughter followed by the thunderous belch of the Gods. Hurriedly, urgently, he makes the sign of the cross in the direction of the men, who seem to unleash unknown forces all around them. They are so few in number, yet so powerful in portent.

Now I feel myself shaking with Asterius, I feel his impulses. His very being is in me, alive, potent. Nothing is asleep, all is awareness. There is a total resurrection of my ancient spirit. My twentieth century being is one with the past. Time is not: I am experiencing another life; another awareness is absorbed and, shaking with excitement, I write; but I am not just the recorder, I am playing my role fully – past and present.

Then I hear a loud, the loudest possible crash of thunder following the very moment where Kerel puts his left foot on the first step of the cathedral, this shrine of Christ. At that instant, the world of Asterius is broken.

Wonder of Wonders!
Miracle of Miracles!
Holy of Holiest Moments in Time!

Another step has been fulfilled. With Kerel, the flow of wisdom from the East, transformed and vitalized by the spiritual experiences of the West, reenters the East. The Ouroboros is complete.

A Change in the Unchangeable!

No one knows what will be brought about next. Strong, Christ-loving Asterius is on his knees. The overwhelming forces of Nature joined with the presence of the four culminate now in a strange and unheard-of spectacle. Out of the church stalks a lion rampant with seven tails and five heads in one. Grabbing Asterius by the shoulders from behind, the Lion raises him off his feet with magic ease and penetrates this saint of the early church with his fiery, life-giving rod. It is a shocking manifestation like those in *Revelations*.

Totally overwhelmed, Asterius leans against his assailant for support. Oh Lord, what next will be demanded of this sturdy soul? The four companions, although they have experienced so much, are in awe of this spectacle. Is this to happen to them? Is this the way to Jerusalem? While they watch and wonder, they see the great majestic Lion turn his prey around to confront the church. Large cracks begin to appear on both sides of the holy edifice, then walls split apart as if they were struck by lightning. Clouds of rose-mauve dust rise all about them, giving the impression of sunset although the sun has barely risen.

Released from the intimate embrace, Asterius is pushed magically into the church toward the altar. Unable to walk, he senses himself floating and freed of the pain in his left thigh which, ever since his torture, has always been part of him. His visitors follow, accustomed by now to broken arches and stones strewn about like pebbles on the beach.

Kerel is deeply impressed by the events. Sensitive François, too much identified with Asterius, is numb and holds his buttocks as if he were the one who had been violated. Walter feels, curiously enough, as if he could understand this symbolic rite, and memories of his black masses well up again. Wilfrid is bewildered, for the faint memory he has of the East, through his former lives, cannot find any echo in this spectacle. But none of them, none of them can remotely evaluate the event.

They are carried along in this terrifying drama of Birth and Rebirth, Death and Life, Darkness and Light. They are all held in the power of the newly emerging God and his enlarged concept of the wholeness of life – not just the spirit of the Father, but that of the Earth-Mother as well; not just one serpent as Redeemer but two serpents, entwined in an eternal Ecstasy of Being; not just the contortions of the One, but the steady rhythms of the Two. This is the uniting of all that was split apart when Lightning rent the veil of the Temple at the time of the Crucifixion. The descent of the Lord is imminent; the Marriage is approaching its fulfillment.

Asterius, followed by the four travelers, moves down the middle aisle. They mount the steps toward the main altar. How many times has the Holy Ghost descended there at that altar into the celebrant of the mass, who, being so imbued, in turn blessed the congregation. This ageless ritual, so familiar to our little group, has been their strength and is the backbone of their spiritual being.

With Kerel in the middle, they form a semicircle in front of the holy place. In anguish, they watch the miraculous disappearance of the altar; instead of the ancient sacrificial table, the Pit of Darkness is revealed, reaching beyond the crypt and into the land of the dead and the damned.

There they see the unlived, the unwanted, that which could not be except in the hopes of mankind, shattered fragments of human attempts, and their willful tragedies. Deeper down the Pit reaches, into all and everything that can be suffered and redeemed by our human psyches. Below that, and beyond reach of any human, lies the unbearable suffering of God for his human race. That is the mysterious dark layer called primordial life which boils up in great bubbles at times with the unmistakable purpose of becoming humanoid, and of starting on the road into human consciousness, where its black pitch must find a way into the suffering awareness leading to its redemption.

How long a road, thinks Kerel, how endless a task! Can we stay alive long enough as a race to suffer that misery? Can my human brain comprehend this road of evolution? He looks at the archbishops, who simply stare, perplexed.

While priests and congregation were receiving the blessings of the one-sided Light of Christ, all that which did not belong to that spiritual kingdom had gone unattended. Spirit, regarded as eternally triumphant, was supreme, and earth cried out in vain. The nether regions were left doomed, locked up, shackled as black pestilence, awaiting the time mankind would be developed enough to comprehend the divinity of All – the Black and the White, the Darkness and the Light – all His creation, for All is sacred in its own way.

As our pilgrims look into the Pit of Eternal Darkness, a lamenting howl softly rises and chills their bones. Raising their hands and eyes for a prayer of mercy, they slowly become aware through the stench, dust, and vapors of the atmosphere that two hands are forming opposite the Pit, full of grace and beauty, unutterably precious and strong. With infinite tenderness, the Left and Right Hands of God move toward each other to unite, and out of this union a ladder is formed, descending deep into the Black. From above, large bitter tears of blood and sorrow begin to fall into the Pit – God's tears shed for man, to resurrect and enliven all that was buried of the human race. Winds of prayer, culminating in a storm, now encircle this divine Pit, as it is not without fear that God encounters his own creation.

"O ye around the Pit ..."

God thunders, even though he tries to whisper in order not to destroy with His immensity,

> "Ye around this Pit of the Unlived,
> Bow your head and pray with Me,
> For here is our fulfillment.
> Out of this womb will rise all
> That is within you
> As you are conceived in My image.

"In My ignorance I brought you here.
Out of ignorance you came here yourselves.
"Receive all this darkness and what it may contain for each of you as My blessing.
"Pray and work for the development of your soul, your soul being the only living creation through which I perceive knowledge of My own Being.
"Bend your knees and know that your divinity is dependent upon your being human.
"Neither plant nor animal can encroach upon Me but through your being. For you are my channel to awareness and greater consciousness of all that is on earth as formed by Me and Me alone."

The village clock of Sils strikes; it is high noon.

Now God's Voice descends to the music of everyday language, all the more devastating and penetrating because of its utter simplicity and matter-of-factness.

"The new day is dawning. Through Me the Christ will be reborn. My only begotten Son will travel into the Greater Light containing the deeper strata of Life's Darkness. And you – Kerel, François, Walter, Wilfrid, Asterius – you are My channel; the development of Christ's church in you is now complete. The time of the Fishes is over. I send you the Waterman, inexperienced but full of new powers and archaic wisdom. Go on your journey to Jerusalem, and see what revelations will come your way. But do not tarry; humanity is waiting."

August 13, 1966
Sils Maria

Humanity can wait.

There they sit on the bank beside the road to Jerusalem; now they are five. How can they travel? So burdened, so heavily burdened! This revelation is hardly to their liking. It is far too unsettling.

Asterius, once so sure of his faith, so eager to welcome his friends, so ready to help them unburden themselves, sits there, perplexed and indignant. The rape has affected him almost more than the revelation of the Pit of Hell and of Unlived Life. His buttocks are sore and his intestines smart from the hot, lava-like substance spurted into him.... "Lord Jesus, what a foul awakening," he thinks. "Is this the spirit of the Pit, this creature from the Bible's *Revelations*? Is it actually alive?" Outraged and furious, he wants to shout, "Revenge, revenge!" But, at that moment, voices of a heavenly choir singing "Hallelujah" intercede and drown out these thoughts. He shakes his head violently and now his body even reacts with delight, and a secret pleasure is in his bowels. What a thing to accept! Then, to his amazement, he has the feeling that he carries the long horn of the Unicorn on his forehead, and his skull tingles slightly at the place where the root would be. He feels his head. Thank God, there is nothing there.

Asterius looks at his companions but meets only Kerel's laughing eyes and a nod which shows he is fully aware of the archbishop's thoughts. A shrug of Asterius' shoulders is the only response. But Kerel, with his ancient mind, knows that the law of opposites is at work. No new Aeon of Aquarius will change that. The Unicorn, a symbol of Christ and His strength, is there at the same time as is the pleasurable feeling in the bowels. Perhaps the New Age will bring a better relationship between the opposites, muses Kerel, thinking of the ladder leading down into the Pit.

Asterius' mind travels back to his Amasia. He stands up to look at his ancient town. It is still there, and he thinks he can perceive the large roof of his church, but not the tower. Is this a trick of his imagination? Will he ever accept the complete debacle and disappearance of his church? He is unable to imagine, as yet, that the landscape is not dominated by his cathedral – all these events are too overwhelming for him. Then, suddenly, his thoughts are pulled back to his belly. What devils and dragons have been created in him, he wonders? He sits down with a loud noise – and that settles that, for the smell is like the breath of the devil. Asterius is undone.

François, always fastidious, looks up amazed at Asterius' lack of manners. With a sigh, he accepts, for isn't this just a minor disturbance? Perhaps his spirit has to become more acquainted with the impact of the opening of the Pit below the altar. "My esthetic being is really my stumbling block," François thinks. "Are the vulgarities of life to be taken less seriously? But what will happen to the delights and grandeur of life? They are so important, for they create an atmosphere in which my spirit can live. What attitude do I take toward that Pit of Hell? Should I be gracious to a pestilent thought? Shall I allow myself to look the monster in the eye and reason with him or it – instead of kicking it back into hell?"

François' entire system seems to be drained; no answer rises up. "Lord knows I have dealt with evil in men and women. How did I ever escape from being devoured by my enemies? I know I created them by being frank and open and as truthful as possible. But truth doesn't always hold wisdom, and it is better silenced so that my tongue won't be cut out."

Bitter worldly thoughts, thoughts of the Pit. François becomes aware that it holds perhaps a great part of his being, and the heavy sadness of silence in his soul weighs him down. Deeper he goes now into those memories of his being which were not allowed to take form or be expressed in words, and created in him a heart so burdened that the simple shock of a carriage accident brought him to his prayerful death. Searching for the soothing comfort of Holy Scripture, he had escaped from the pain of his being. Indeed he knows now that he has a Pit in himself.

"What else will be brought up that I haven't already met?" he asked himself. "I remember writing once near my end: 'I think I have no desire to taste of the world. It seems as if there is a barrier between it and me, which prevents any longing on my part and which would, I fancy, stand not a little in my way were I, one day, called upon to return to it.'"

Walter and Wilfrid are holding hands; no, Walter's hand is resting on Wilfrid's. The two men from York know much about the Pit and shudder at the thought of having to deal with all that devilish black part of life again.

After a while, Walter gets up and moves away from his companions. He looks at the other side of the bank. There, behind a dry moat, rises a wall with a single window. Is it a castle? In the window sits the nubile maiden, Miriam. She sits and spins and sings an endless song to hide the pain within. It is not a lament – it is the song of Not Knowing what is or has been.

Walter looks up at her, waves and is noticed. Smilingly, she waves back and puts her spindle aside. She smiles in her own way the smile of a woman who has suffered beyond endurance, longer than can be known. One who is made to suffer, she is – and because of that, incredibly beautiful to man's soul. She leans out of the window: "I might perhaps come down to you, men, for I know your fate and I know you as harbingers of freedom of spirit."

Walter raises his eyebrows in surprise and smiles at this turn of events. He answers: "Soul travelers, we are, in search of Jerusalem, the City of the Golden Heart." What makes me say that? he wonders.

"I know. I know you are right. Christ is waiting.

The City of God will open its gate wide, but it will not be the way you expect it. Tarry a while and I will join you, from beyond this moat separating Life from Death. I too will be on my way. I have been sitting here an aeon – waiting-waiting-waiting endlessly, waiting for the end of time. Don't be upset if I cry as I appear: it will be from happiness as well as grief, the same pain we all experience at every birth." She disappears, throwing a kiss to Walter.

Have the others seen this? Yes, Kerel has, of course; the others were all too preoccupied with their own thoughts and the black hole under and beyond the altar of Christianity.

Here she comes, clutching her skirts to free the path for her feet. Both hands hold up the coarsely woven material. She goes straight to Walter, makes her little curtsy and says calmly: "Don't worry, only Kerel and you can see me. Like you, I have come a long way, but my way through the ages was one of observing – no acting, only painfully observing the fate of the mute women, the God-bearing pregnant women. Part of God is in all men. I have always known that I am not the only God-bearing woman. I am Miriam, the Virgin. Isha Jahu had me in mind when, seven centuries before, he prophesied the birth of Emmanuel. He is my son. In Isha's being I was formed; his spirit carried silently the immensity of the suffering woman-spirit in humanity. It is because of him that I survived. It is because of him that there was comfort at all."

With eyes almost glazed, she continues: "I heard time and time again, 'Comfort ye, comfort ye!' The Lord of Hosts in his mightiness eyes the sufferer as his jewel; then I would have peace, until the spasms of agony in human existence convulsed my wretched woman's soul. Oh, how I would echo painfully to the heart-strings of my true being."

"The Divine, having foreseen and foretold the muting of women's voice, enthroned me as a symbol of divine virtue without ever giving me the chance to speak or commune. I am the symbol of silent Death; the howling note of cosmic suffering is heard in my heart. I carry the cosmic pain, that is why all people come to me, for silent understanding and mute strength. In my frail unformed body, I formed the body of the Man Who carried out the spoken message and Who enacted the divine drama with His disciples. But I was mute, my song not heard, so, in the subterranean passages of life, as if in a maze, I moved unheard. Some of the church builders knew it in their hearts, and pictured my path on their church floors where, like me, men and women would crawl on their knees through the maze for absolution and to pacify their grief. But unnoticed, silently, my spirit crept all over the world. Kwan Yin – Maria – whatever name was given me represents the feminine mercy of God's Being."

Miriam sighs now and smiles again, but much more brightly. "The spirit of the comforter is returning, Walter, with you and your friends. He will know about my new road and, like a cosmic pawn, the stars will move me to my new bridegroom. When He is ready, He will again open my womb but, this time, also my lips. What will escape, what will be first, the Lord only knows, but I will have a voice. My belly rumbles already and the earth is agitated, and now I am shaking – SHAKING, do you hear?" She shouts "shaking" and emits a fearful belch which awakens every one of our travelers out of his reverie. No one sees her, for she is swallowed up by the tree, against which she had put her hand to steady her shaking, shaken self. But now the earth shakes and shakes and ripples the countryside.

"The Virgin's healing breasts," cries Kerel, all of a sudden.

"No, her God-bearing belly," answers Walter, and the others, simply bewildered by these explosive words, watch as the road moves like the waves of an ocean. And the rounding movement of the earth is as the breasts and belly of the Virgin, and everywhere there is a fragrance as of orchids, and the love for God is like an explosive dynamism in the soul of the travelers, for now they are all standing and being moved toward their goal; they gasp for air, and each gasp is like the wine of life as they come nearer the seat of their soul. Divinely drunk, they stare ahead as the undulating earth directs them towards Jerusalem. The road moves them as if they were floating on an ocean's groundswell. Jerusalem is not drawing them so much as the earth is pushing them toward the City.

Behind their backs, the tree brings forth Miriam again, and she joins with the unseen but ever-present rear guard. The Prince of Light and the Prince of Darkness have been slowly walking their straight path toward Jerusalem. They, too, go toward their destiny and will wait in the garden of the Holy Temple until they are called to enter. They go slowly, for Miriam's spirit is like lead. Two thousand years of pain are carried by the adolescent woman. The Virginal Maiden wonders about so many things as she leans heavily on her companions. At times, her knees buckle. She is now at the end of her road. A few more steps and she will find relief. "Can I make it, now that relief is in sight?" She does not seem to care at this moment. "Forward, forward," she hears from somewhere. Her legs move, her hands press on her heart. The load is too heavy. All humanity's wounded love is upon her. "Like an Atlas, I have to be," she exclaims, and stops. "I can't collapse now. Where will I find the strength to go on?"

A cry of agonized surprise makes her look up. The wayfarers have reached their goal, and, oh my God, it is not Jerusalem, but the square beak of an enormous monster which is about to swallow them up. The agony in Wilfrid's backward glance helps Miriam. He throws out his right arm in a plea, for they are entering the beak of the monster. It is the plea for help which gives her life, strength. So, with her smile of beatitude, she waves back and automatically fulfills her eternal role of Man's support in distress. But this time, she knows that it is not a son calling on her, but a man, a mature, warmhearted man, who knows suffering, and it awakens in her the woman-mate, the companion, the co-traveler in the cosmic maze.

Then, with an enormous throaty gurgle, the monster passes our pilgrims through the gateway beak right into the center of Jerusalem.

After thousands of years of human effort and struggle with divine destiny, the City of God, the new Jerusalem, has come to Earth. The promised land is now open to all, even unto Moses.

Jerusalem! Cool air, magnificent atmosphere, crystal clearness all around; our wayfarers stand awed, overwhelmed by the immensity of the love of God surging through them. It is as if an electric shock had stunned them. Soon, however, rather too soon, the five travelers recover their senses. The critical mind, with all the limitations it suffers when confronted with the unknown, begins to work in François. With French disdain, he says: “Eh bien, this does not mean anything. Somewhere there will be foul play.” Walter is pleased, relieved perhaps to have a short breathing space, while Wilfrid swallows the whole experience with delight. Asterius says with great feeling: “Bah, we will be fooled again,” but he is glad of the respite. Kerel simply observes the beautiful marketplace, hub of all spirituality, and now completely empty except for our wayfarers. All is absolutely quiet, as if humanity had deserted the City of Redemption.

The silence is broken by a rhythmic tapping. Our pilgrims turn and see a beggar with a cane coming toward them from a side street. Kerel knows him; the others recall him faintly. Yes, he is one of them: their first Christian ancestor, Judas Barsabas, son of a wealthy tentmaker of the tribe of Judah and a prophet in his own right. Schooled and trained in the Greek tradition, he is a highly civilized man who helped Paul and Silas bring the teachings of Jesus, the Christ, to the gentiles of Antioch. Judas is bent and tired today because, in spite of his convictions, a restless mental activity forces him to probe constantly into the mysteries of life.

“You’re all back,” he says, “in this glorious town in which I am a beggar.” He looks at all his descendants: so there they are, they have come home. He welcomes them all. The travelers are now quick to recognize him and encircle him warmly, feeling their affiliation with this quizzical-looking man. They stare intensely at him and he at them without speaking a word. Only the eyes are communicating, and, through this curious language, springs a greater awareness. They sense that they are all one, and that Judas is the original Christian in their family.

Barsabas is proud of what has developed out of his soul: priests and wise men. He knows this could have happened only on account of that one moment of full comprehension he experienced when he visited the field of Golgotha where Christ was crucified. Barsabas' spirit wants to travel back to the great events of the past, but this is not the time for it. So, gathering himself to face the present moment, he says with a slightly mysterious smile: "My wife knows that you are here and has sent me to welcome you. She is All that is, both Witch and Angel, and even God mirrors himself in Her. I wonder in what state she will receive you."

As Judas turns to lead his guests toward his crystal house situated right in front of them on the square, a terrific gust of wind whips away the curtain in front of the entrance and reveals a beautiful warm hall with red carpets – a lovely welcome to the fatigued travelers. Judas invites them all in: "This is my wife's home, where I live most of the time," he says. "She sends her love and will see you when you are refreshed, bathed, and ready for dinner."

At long last the wayfarers have arrived. This is their house, their home. Overwhelmed and exhausted, they enter.

August 14, 1966
Sils Maria

"Why are you a beggar?" asks Wilfrid, when they are refreshed and reunited in the Hall.

"This life is my doom as well as my reward," answers Judas. "For I am always too mental, not accepting life as it is. Through begging I learn to take what is given me and to live accordingly. When I rebel, I go hungry, and my misery leads me to acceptance once again. When I accept my state of mind, whatever it is, I am provided for, and then I automatically return to this house which is my home. But I do rebel, and I doubt. But that too is a blessing, for then I learn and often get to know more than my wife who sits here in her eternal bliss." Judas thinks of his sweet Sophia and smiles. His wife is a very complicated lady. "She knows that my rebellion is also a pilgrimage, and that my experience adds to her wisdom, although she hates to admit it and becomes a real she-devil when I tell her a few home truths which she doesn't know yet. Being married to a Goddess, a High Priestess, is sheer hell for my human side, but bliss in the time between my pilgrimages. And so we are united with the strongest ties."

Then he silences his tongue. "What now?" he wonders. "What will I do? Do they know that Sophia is also God's wife? Will they be upset knowing I am married to God in a tripartite? How will Sophia welcome them? What aspect of the Wisdom of God will she reveal?"

There is no smile left on Judas' lips now that the moment of confrontation has arrived. It is as if a black hand gently grips his golden heart as he senses that the purpose of the long trek from York to Jerusalem nears its climax.

Suddenly a blast of heavenly trumpets sounds and blends into one note, transforming Judas into a divine pawn who majestically turns around to lead the way to the north wall of the Hall. A round door appears and opens slowly. Our pilgrims follow Judas in single file through this "Breathing Hole of Eternity." It is a solemn procession, and each of them feels the momentous occasion.

Now they are six – six, the number of blackness and dynamic power, but also the human expression of the Trinity. So they enter. "Oh, God, what now?" A fearful shudder goes through them. Their skin prickles; their backbones tingle as they experience the atmosphere of this most holy room. What they see is a simple setting for an evening supper, arranged on a plain table. Some see a cloth, others a cleanly scrubbed surface.

But who is seated there? It is not a woman, not a man. Facing them is the very spirit of an immense Idea, the stark simplicity of the Christ in its most awesome form. Is this Judas' wife? There is light all around, in that mysterious fashion one experiences in dreams. They all realize and know that this will be their Last Supper. Two thousand years have passed, and now at the end of time, it is as at the beginning. Then, the Piscean myth descended to earth; only now can they experience the myth in its totality, thus rounding out the old and starting the new in the psyche of all mankind. Deep down in their being, the six recognize that they are descendants also of Peter and Paul, and they look for their friends – John, Matthew, Mark and Thomas – with whom they shared their experiences. Is Stephen far away? And Andros, where is he? They all seem to be there, but unseen.

The Man of Light rises calmly, and Judas introduces each of the wayfarers by his first name. The Man nods and says: "You seem familiar to me. In fact, I remember most of what you did in your lifetimes." Then he sits down, motioning to his guests to do likewise. As they are being seated by Judas, the light of Christ's face changes and becomes warm and human.

"I am Jesus of Nazareth," he says simply, breaking the bread and pouring the wine. He looks at the men kindly and drinks. All raise their glasses, and some tears drop into the wine. Walter chokes, and part of his wine spills out of his mouth onto the table.

"Bless you, Walter, you choke on your Black Mass, don't you?" Jesus asks.

The shock of drinking with Christ Jesus is too much for Walter. And so he reacts in a most primitive and vicious manner.

"No. On you. Who do you say you are?"

"Jesus of Nazareth," is the calm answer.

"Where is the Christ?" Walter asks brusquely, shocking the others.

"In you and me," He answers.

"Sure, sure, I know. And His Shadow?" Walter persists.

"In you and me," comes the reply.

"You are damned right," says Walter. "In me and in you." He looks ahead, staring into space, remembering the endless suffering he has undergone at his own death and the acceptance of his duality and all that is in him. He hears bells ring and toll.

At this very moment, in actuality,
I hear the bells start to ring here in Sils Maria
on this Sunday morning.

An aeon of suffering sweeps through Walter, which gives him strange strength. He stands up calmly, walks from his bench toward Jesus and puts his arms around him. They kiss and embrace.

The others do not understand what is happening. They do not comprehend that this is Walter's moment of complete acceptance of his Black Mass. He has suffered it, and so has Jesus. This mutual experience has broken the spell of awe in Walter. He recognizes that Jesus is not the Christ of two thousand years ago, but that unbelievably mature, wise man who has realized what has happened in the last aeon. Walter senses you can be intimate with this man, you can love his warmth, as long as you remain connected with your own warmth and do not cheat your human side.

Then Jesus turns to Walter and says: "Look!" He shows him two fangs protruding from his mouth. Walter takes one fang in his hand, shakes it slightly and says with a sigh and so sadly: "Yes, do I know! Yes, indeed." He then shows his own menacing teeth. Walter's hand now clasps the hand of Jesus the Christ and thus they sit sadly together for a while. A deep tie of mutual and painful experience seems to forge them together. There is no difference at this moment between Christ Jesus and Christ Walter.

"What can develop now?" Judas wonders, watching them all. Kerel, with head in hand, is toying with the bread and turning his wine glass. François doesn't understand the bond between Walter and Jesus. He hears the strains of a music incomprehensible to him as yet, a cadence totally foreign to his seventeenth-century ear. It chills his bones and, to warm himself, he gathers his train around his feet. They are freezing. He realizes how far he has journeyed from his stately Court into the present setting of timeless simplicity. Closing his eyes, he prays fervently to the Almighty for comfort and understanding.

Wilfrid looks astonished, only faintly comprehending the new alliance between Jesus and Walter. With his right hand, he reaches for Asterius' comforting presence, but Asterius is only half there. He is deeply withdrawn and in a state of shock brought on by the relentless assault of devastating events with which he has had to cope. Judas, much worried, sees Asterius float away in a cloud of despair. Trying to get him back, Judas sends him all his love and affection, but apparently Asterius can return only when he becomes willing to weep uncontrollably. He is floating back into the front hall to grasp the one pillar that is there; and then, without a sob or a sound, the tears start to pour. He is so sad, so terribly upset. He had seen the protruding fangs in both men, and that mutual recognition which seems so important to Walter and Jesus is just hideous to him. Judas, who has gone begging so many times, excuses himself from the table and goes to the hall to console Asterius and bring him back into his own. He puts his arm around the shocked Bishop of Amasia and walks back and forth with him in front of the unlit hearth.

"Beloved brother, don't try to hold back your sobs. To see the duality of Jesus Christ is frightening. At first, I saw only His Shadow and had trouble seeing His Light. I knew Jesus before the days he was the Christ, and I didn't really accept His mission until I experienced what happened at the Cross, the terrible marriage between the human-animal or animal-human side and the presence of God, a moment of death, oblivion and tearing apart – a rending departure into the heavens of God's spirit which has walked the earth, and a new spiritual union between God and Man prevailed."

Judas sighs as he contemplates whether he should continue to relate his experiences. The need of the moment decides, thus he continues: "I didn't follow all the teachings of Jesus, and especially not those of His disciples. I did experience, however, that dreadfully important moment when God is Christ, Jesus and Man, all united in an embrace so that nothing more exists but their power inalienably together, forever. Something happened, not just there on the hill of Golgotha, but everywhere in the cosmos. At the instant of that union, activated by the Holy Ghost, a reality became available to all mankind."

Asterius only nods; he needs to hear a sympathetic voice. "Just talk, just talk to me, Judas," he pleads. Judas is only too glad to continue; he senses that he has never spoken so fully from his heart.

"Registering this divine drama was most difficult for me and nearly cost me my life. For years after that experience, I was frail. The marrow of my bones was almost burned out by the searing fire of God's presence. It is only in that burning supreme moment that there is Absolute Union." He pauses and continues. "Later on, many have suffered similar experiences, and Walter came close to it at his death. A priceless gift was waiting for him. He was old and tired from his work, and his ego was no longer dominant. Only then was he prepared to enter into a union with his Self. On his deathbed, he could suffer the pain of his power-drunk blackness which, to his astonishment, brought about a clear vision and contact with his innermost being. Through his suffering, he recognized an aspect of the Light in his own darkness. He never forgot this. The revelation of the evil fangs shows the hard road we have to travel to come to a fuller comprehension of our duality. This is the basis of the understanding that exists between Jesus and Walter."

Asterius senses the warmth of Judas' feeling, which is so reassuring, but he finds it hard to accept the idea that Light can be reached through the darkness of evil. He can only vaguely compare the suffering of Walter with that of the redeemed thief on the cross. His heart reacts, for he feels that Judas speaks with love and true wisdom, the wisdom of personal experience – an idea lived, not just comprehended. "The Inner Light comes from the experience suffered," Judas adds.

Judas' revelatory account and the love that has brought it about pull like a magnet and bring Jesus out into the hall. He speaks in a trancelike state: "That was beautifully put, Judas. Blessings on all those who know; in them the Christ lives and His glory will flow for ever and ever." Shaking himself more awake from the deep memories of the past, he continues: "You brought Golgotha here out of love for Asterius. Now tell us about your conversion as we sit around the hearth. I will light the fire."

As Jesus lights the fire, our companions enter the hall to take their proper places. Kerel sits to the left of Judas and Jesus sits on his right side. These three are the center of the group. Asterius sits next to Jesus with François at his side. Sitting at Kerel's left is Walter, with Wilfrid next to him completing a half moon. With the crescent-shaped hearth, the magic circle is formed.

In this completion something is still missing however, which is not apparent to those present. While they are seven, the three in the middle are truly one, the oneness of the Christian Ancestor, Judas Barsabas, who sits with the four companions forming the five so that both the seven and the five are represented, creating the twelve. Of the original thirteen, one is still missing and that one awaits redemption.

It is as if I am number thirteen. Am I the one to be redeemed? And who then will be my redeemer? Or is number thirteen the redeemer who will bring about the magic in my soul? I have been listening to these inner voices and my pen could not stop writing. So there they sit in the cave of my heart. Christ is now included in the twelve. What or who will be thirteen? I listen and look, and see that all are seated in their proper places. There is a quiet as if each were entering himself by watching the fire. Out of this silence, Judas' story of Golgotha wells up. Directing his words to the flames, he begins his reminiscences with difficulty and hesitation.

"I went to the Cross where Christ Jesus met with destiny. It was some weeks after the actual crucifixion and after my sickness that I dared to show openly any interest in the life of the Nazarene. I knew of Jesus and had heard about him through my emotional brother, Joseph; he was almost chosen as a disciple to replace my namesake, Judas, who had to pay with his life for his treachery. I never liked that man Iscariot and could not see why such a creature was ever elected to be one of the so-called chosen ones. If Jesus was such a great soul or man, how could he ever associate with people like that? Yet there had gathered around him many intelligent and worthwhile beings who, although perhaps not too worldly or wise, could not be led astray so easily – and I still shake my head as I attempt to comprehend how that curious group of disciples was selected.

"Now, as I think back, I feel as if the Twelve plus Jesus were a divine unit – a band, a group of souls willing to take on and live a message, a myth. Each of them was part of the divine plan, each life being able to represent an archaic symbol in the flesh. That myth was a brutal performance of divine power, a rape of human beings obeying the New Dawn – just as the other day when you, Asterius, now, at the end of time, were so cruelly shocked by another divine power, the King of the Beasts."

Shifting in his chair and crossing his legs, he continues, rather matter-of-factly: "You know, of course, there is a great complication with a living Christ and a man like Jesus; then, also, there is my own complication over how I thought about Him while He lived and later, how I felt about Him after the crucifixion with its amazing resurrection. It is so difficult to tell you about those times, as they are now two thousand years ago. I was different, then, harder, more intellectual and slightly arrogant. Thus I could never think of Jesus as King of the Jews. I knew too many inappropriate little details of his life ever to think of him that way. I had met Him, and while one side of me was rather favorably impressed, my deep inner being must have been profoundly affected. You might say that in one way my attitude was condescending, but in another way it was very respectful. A remarkable curiosity was kindled in me after each encounter. Slight as that sometimes was, it always required a moment of meditation to figure Him out.

"You know, like so many of my friends, I was not a devout Jew. Although we learned about the teachings of Isaiah and the prophets, it was more fashionable and cultured to be conversant with the Greek philosophers and to follow the Roman civilization. But in spite of these cultural involvements, I have a mystical side which at that time was very embarrassing to me. That irrational part of my nature relentlessly pushed me on and on and brought about a restless spirit. Moods of irony and irritation often came over me, and it was in these difficult times that I heard about the Sermon on the Mount at Capernaum. I was not there but was told about it in glowing terms by my brother, Joseph, whom I love very much. He was willing to accept a road from which I shied away. Joseph impressed me, though, and the reaction caused by Jesus' words among His listeners was formidable. Although

I could not get a clear account of everything that was said, it seemed to me the people were all inspired. A flow of something, an emanation, must have come forth from Jesus which was almost too powerful for them to handle. There was a 'silent' hysteria among the crowd, which to me is a typical sign of the presence of a power greater than can be understood.

"Now that was the thing that attracted me immensely, although I never said so. This living unseen quality – this true spirit of God in a man – was what I hungered for. I did not want to go with it, but it was working in my brother and others who followed the Christ. I, by trying to undo and depreciate this quality, seemed to act like a poker stirring a fire, stimulating them still more. I secretly loved doing this, for it really proved that they were possessed by an unconquerable spirit, an inflamed psyche which, although they could not handle it intelligently, was left undaunted by my skepticism."

Judas pauses for a moment. The spell of the fire is working its way but, anxious to forestall the painful crux of his story, he tries to take his time. The inevitable reliving of the past is closing in on him, and he wonders if he will experience the accompanying agony again. He looks around at the circle in the hall, but there is no forestalling. The inner voice of memory takes over and he continues:

"My contact with Jesus was more from afar. The few times I met him, he extended just the polite, civil behavior granted to older people. I was about twenty years his senior. Jesus never tried to influence me, nor was he influenced by my social standing or riches. The fatal story of the end which all of you have preached so many times came during the Passover. Oh my God, I stayed away from it all. It made me sick with anxiety, so sick, in fact, that I could not celebrate this day of the Egyptian miracle when the blood of the Lamb was stronger than pestilence. What sign on our lintel could now again bring such salvation?

"Then I remembered an ominous dream in which I saw the red smear of blood of the Lamb form itself into a shimmering cross, which became a living, pulsating horror against a dark cloud. A star pierced this horrible vision. My soul shrieked out: 'What sacrifice and doom will come to us?' I awoke with a shock, mumbling, 'Oh, my people, my people.' My thoughts were fixed on the Babylonian exile and whether Isaiah would rise again to comfort us.

"I pushed the dream aside as being too nightmarish. The drama around me and this dream were very baffling. I possessed no insight to clarify my mind."

Judas moves around, shifts his legs and looks at his open palms; then slowly he rubs his right middle finger in a circle on his left hand, not speaking for a while. Then, talking to himself as if becoming aware for the first time, he continues:

"Unknown to myself, I was being imbued by the majesty of Christ's Being. This was the most uncanny thing of all because, looking at Him, I could see that He was very much like us. But there is in my memory of Him a magic which worked on me and everyone He met; they experienced either an uncontrollable hatred and contempt, or a deeper and deeper love toward Him and concern for their own soul.

"I took to my bed, sick and feverish from what I had heard. I was hopelessly involved in the cataclysm of the last days and, in spite of my high fever, begged everyone for information. No one could understand the reason for my anxious questioning, least of all my family. I was considered too worldly, too well balanced to show any interest in the doings of this rebellious upstart. But my spirit was in agony. I was like a house divided; the love of intellect and the love of spirit were in a deadly duel. That was the reason for my fever. The spirit penetrated and won, and I knew I had to go to the place of the supreme sacrifice: Golgotha." Then, with a deep sigh, he paused.

The next day,
I wrote:

So I went. It was a good clear day, and the scene I knew so well was undisturbed. Nothing was new; nothing was different – Nature lives on: the last spring flowers, the beginning of summer. The vineyards, they would do well on a day like this. All went its own way, following the endless cycle of spring, summer, fall, winter, spring, summer, fall, winter. The change was in me. The change was in me!

It is obvious that Judas is marking time, unwilling to relive the experience of his conversion. Indeed, Judas is thinking: Will I be capable of handling that terribly gripping experience again? He looks at his companions, his travel companions in life. Will his conversion be shattered the way their churches were, their immense cathedrals, their palaces? He looks around his own Hall. Will this go, too? Jesus, sitting next to him, doesn't smile; neither does Kerel. As Jesus stares into the fire, Kerel looks toward Judas. There is anticipation, understanding and encouragement in his look. So Judas continues:

"I came to the crosses; three perpendicular beams standing like stripped trees. Only some wildflowers waving innocently in the wind were there now, my witnesses on the field of Golgotha. I knelt next to the tree in the center – denuded of branch and victim – where the great union had taken place.

"As I went deeper into prayer, the magic of the soil, the power of the Cross and the heavenly spirit united in me, and, sobbing, I fell to the ground. 'Never, never more, oh Lord, will I put my mind against Thee.' I felt the utter smallness of my being and the immensity of the Divine Spirit. I dedicated my Self, my soul, my total being to His service. Never again would I do other than follow my own path as Jesus had followed His.

"I surrendered completely to the spirit of God, and at that horrible divine moment, something tore in my flesh as if my belly, my guts were being separated from my heart. From then on, I could follow only the world of my heart. Spirit would reign supreme – and all that which belongs to flesh would have to be denied. How could that be? I would live without earth, which is God's creation also. Would I ever succeed? It was like a curse.

"For a moment, I thought: Is this a curse like that on Judas Iscariot? Have I betrayed the Lord, too? But a voice in me said: 'No, dearly beloved Son of Man, this is the price to pay for your surrender. You will have to live more like a spirit than like a man in order to become the Son of God. This is the aeon of Christ, which will lead man further on his quest toward self-awareness. Your spirit will be as wine to mankind; your example will be as living bread. At all times, Spirit will have to conquer blood and flesh. Go among men, not just to teach the Gospel, but to be a man in Christ's spirit. By living in this manner you preach the Gospel. Then the Word will flow from you and you will speak as a beloved son. Through all the changes to come, there will be no change in our bondage until you and your progeny are gathered together at the end of time to unite in My house."

The prophetic inner voice of Judas of two thousand years ago has become the reality of the Now. The entire company has the same thought, the realization that they are one. They have traveled a long, hard road, alone apparently – but now they are home. They look at one another – Christ, Kerel, Judas, François, Walter, Asterius and Wilfrid. Asterius tries to fade away into his own time. Christ, aware of his neighbor's evasive mood, puts his arm gently around him and so forces him to participate in what is happening.

At that, a clap of thunder announces the nearness of the Dark Brother. With lightning speed, the whole memory of the last two thousand years passes through their minds. Their suffering, their unmarried state, their desperate efforts to withstand the denial of the flesh – all is registered with the fierce pain brought about when the essence of ourselves is touched. Their love is for a God as presented by Jesus the Christ. The hermaphroditic power in this magnificent God-man is the terrible anchor of their masculinity. This is what they faintly realized when they entered the dining hall and were greeted by the figure of Christ instead of Judas' wife.

Kerel now addresses his beloved sons: "Oh, priests of the past, what cruelty you carry. In the cosmic cycles, each aeon brings its sacrifices and its rewards. As men, your feminine spirit had to be carried by the hermaphroditic Christ. You have fulfilled your task and gathered great wisdom with the endless pain created by the spirit as the answer to all. Await now your moment of deliverance and watch him who has led you before." Christ looks away, shaken. The time of His purity is past. Total clarity of Being penetrates Him. He knows, now, all about the tragedy of the separation, the tearing apart in the body of the two Judases – Judas Iscariot the betrayer, the one who had to live in the nether world, and Judas Barsabas, the converted, who had to live in the world of spirit. Who had suffered more, he wonders? But wouldn't both have their place of love in the eyes of God? Didn't both represent the human suffering? Didn't both fulfill their destiny? One went the way of the earth and its riches – the other the way of the spirit and the heavens. Christ falls down on His knees. The thunder rumbles. The City of God shakes, the Beloved Son is in agony: HE PRAYS:

> "Oh, God, send greater wisdom to Me. In the mirror of time, I see the Betrayer, the Betrayed and My followers. We all play the part You assign to us, oh Lord. We are the actors who obey Your Creation. Good or bad, we obey. Lord, restore the soul of Judas who betrayed. Bless the soul of Judas who sacrificed his human nature to be Your priest.
> Lord God, recognize Your own Wholeness,
> gather unto Yourself all that is, all of Your Creation,
> to enter the New Era.
> Lord, let me die.
> For I am not worthy of Your Wholeness.
> Grant me this wish and restore the powers of Your fullness.
> Create again and anew and be aware.
> The world awaits Your Word.
> Give us new tongues with which to speak.

Bless Kerel and grant him Your new Powers.
Wholeness, O Lord!
Your Humanity, Your World Soul is at stake.
Kerel, Asterius, Wilfrid, Walter, François, Judas Barsabas,
All in Erlo we are united.
Grant us, oh Lord, the privilege to live our lives
with grace, beauty and integrity.
Give us the strength to carry self-awareness and
bring that jewel to Your Throne."

As the Christ stands up, the Heavens release the New Music of the spheres which opens, with unseen hands, the closed doors to the Dining Hall. Bathed in a Light resplendent stands the Woman Spiritual, the Wife of God, Mother to All and Companion to the Christ, the soul of all men – the Anima Mundi!

Happily smiling and radiant, Sophia nears slowly. At the same time, unnoticed by our group, the main door of the Hall to the marketplace opens slightly, and through the crack Judas Iscariot enters. Only Christ Jesus is aware, through the tingling of his spine, that the betrayer is approaching. His Dark Brother comes closer, closer and gently, very gently, Judas enters Jesus through the backbone. This union carries the same power and feeling as an oncoming orgasm. In that final mingling of both pain and delight, they face each other. Unutterable love flows between the two as they fuse. In an explosion of Light their forces unite. So blinding is the moment that no one sees for a while. The Anima Mundi shudders in ecstasy. Her moment is here. She gives birth; She receives; She is All – She is Whole, Supreme and fully aware. Only She reigns. It is the moment of earth's magic, Spirit and Matter are one. Blindness is in the group. There is no Jesus, no Judas; instead, there is the newly born, inexperienced young man, Mr. Waterman – the divine Aquarius.

In that supreme moment of blinding Light, the Great Mother opens Her robes wide, and with an agonizing shriek which She has held back since the time of the Crucifixion, She brings forth Miriam, the beautiful bride and mate to Aquarius. Now She comes from out of the Mother, the Eternal Feminine, always there, always present but not always seen, as Her form belongs to the mystery of life.

Miriam comes toward Aquarius hesitatingly. Now that the moment is here for the encounter with the new groom, she trembles, she blushes, she senses the overpowering presence of the Great Mother. It gives her strength to go ahead, to enter life anew and differently from before. The step is great. "Will the moon still be under my feet? Will the rays of the Divine Presence still emanate as before? Will the sword still be directed toward my heart?"

All these thoughts storm her brain. Then, with a peal of laughter like crystal bells announcing the union, she shakes off all her virginal symbols. The Pietàs all over creation glow, and Christ the Son looks up at his Mother, smiles, and walks away without wounds.

Wedding bells ring. Miriam begins to speak: "Aquarius, my Lord and Mate, Servant of my Love, King of my heart, and Slave to the Divine demands of our union, here I am, like you ready for the marriage chamber. The Heavens have spoken, and as you came out of the Union of Christ and His Shadow, so I appeared through this union in Jerusalem. What a road lies ahead of us! What Heavenly or Hellish design may or will be our destiny! We will carry it together. No more will I wander alone in the Valley of Death. We will call on the Spirit Divine. We are the Spirit Divine of the Eternal Union between man and woman: female and male revealed or not revealed. We can unite at long last: we are the Union of all opposites."

Ecstatically, she falls into the arms of the astonished Aquarius; but this contact comes like an electric shock to Aquarius' body, an awakening of all that had slumbered. His potential is vitalized, his energies awaken. "Oh, my love," he says, "my love, my love, I didn't know who you were when I saw you; neither could I imagine the feelings in my heart and being caused by your presence. My God, I am home. I have a home on earth." And leaning on each other as if that would forever secure their happiness, they approach the Great Mother.

The Anima Mundi, looking at their happiness with her clear eyes, breaks out with agonizing joy: "Oh, my God, I am being pulled into human consciousness!" Fear appears in her eyes. Is she losing her divinity? No loss – she is gaining in humanity. She prays: "May my children not suffer any more in vain, but comprehend the meaning of their pain."

"Mother Goddess," speaks Aquarius, "this is my wedding gift to you. I promise that in my reign your sons and daughters will not be killed for their new ways of thought and ideals. My protection will always be there, even when the Darkness envelops them; and, as they address themselves to me, I will manifest the Light which the Christ initiated through his birth in Jesus. The suffering of your people – your children – brought me the Light of Lucifer. His Light and Christ's Light will at all times be my inseparable companions. Thus I will fulfill my dual nature."

A deep curtsy without words is the answer of the most powerful of all powers on earth, from whose womb life has started.

Miriam then speaks, looking down on her hands enfolded with those of Aquarius: "Beloved Mother, whose role I fulfilled unto the most excruciating pain of my Being, I will now go on a different road. Hard though it may be, I will not be alone, and my gift to you is that, in this happy moment, I dedicate my life, my marriage to filling the hearts of humanity with the Love I gave my firstborn an aeon ago. May our marriage be the symbol of union everywhere."

At that, a clap of thunder rolls over the mountains, here in the Engadine.

Now my beloved incarnations all form a circle and dance rhythmically. They know their end is here – the end of their Piscean era. Love flows among them! They have succeeded, each in his own task. The New is born out of the Old. Nothing is lost. All has been assimilated so that the magic birth could take place. Asterius is happy as he feels the primitive and the spiritual coming together. Judas Barsabas feels the healing of his wounds. Wilfrid drops his life's burden of squabbling and trail-blazing; his job is done. Walter is freed of his guilt and is joyous. He knows that his blackness is completely redeemed. François dances, deeply contented. After the fearful journey with its sublime ending, he knows that he can have what was always deep within him, the contact with the seer. There is a fulfillment of the past which carries with it the seed and essence of the future.

We all dance together and, from their hearts, they tell me they will follow me, Erlo, the scribe, the stage, and the actor. Each slowly enters me in deep rest and contentment, and all will hopefully live harmoniously within my soul, ready to start our New Life.

Sophia, in the doorway, waits for Aquarius and Miriam, who stand in front of the fire started by the Christ. They are only half aware of what goes on. Great expectations for the aeon to come, hope in humanity, and trust in God make them happy.

Kerel prays that the marriage of Miriam and Aquarius will be fruitful for the world, and we join in fervent prayer that we may understand our newly acquired femininity, love it, cherish it and live with it until death do us part.

I, Erlo, sit in my chair next to the window in the Waldhaus of Sils Maria. The thunder is still in the distance. It is raining now, so there is *Tao*. My body aches; there seems to be no rest in me, although my psyche is at peace. More work is still to be done.

The last thunder has just rolled away over the mountain peaks.

Part II

August 16, 1966
Sils Maria

Snowing on the mountains. Raining in the valley.
The day after the Union.

Last night, the magical birth of Aquarius and Miriam was read to my wife, and now I will have to wait and see if anything wants me to write further. I look out of the window towards the mountains and all seems so peaceful, despite the stormy atmosphere. Suddenly, I hear clearly a voice from within – but I refuse to write down what it says. Bosh! It is rot, it stinks – it is a message of such self-glorification that I can't bear to go on. Then the inner ear registers the words: "You had better listen, for the archetypes do not talk in small terms – they are Gods. You had better obey – you know that you always get sick or get into trouble when you don't go with your inner voices. Listen to them. Write down what they say – and let the chips fall where they may. But don't obstruct; for you it is dangerous. Let go. Let go."

I sigh, knowing full well that my unconscious is right. Here goes, so help me God. May I dare to write what comes up from the depths of my being.

A shiver goes through me. "Erlo, it is up to you now; never did I think you would come to grips in such an astounding way with your past lives. That was a very tough accomplishment. This is the World Anima speaking, who will be stern with you. I can teach you, but I also realize that you can teach me. Unbelievable vistas have opened which startle even me, your teacher and companion, so that I can comprehend things now with greater clarity and perception. Erlo, you are at a turning point. You are dedicated to the Waterman, just as you were dedicated to the Piscean Christ – the Divine Fisherman. Now, in the name of young Aquarius, you are to live in the New Age as his example. You have to write the first leading account in Aquarius' chronicle. Don't shake your head – just listen. The moment is important.

"You are a manifestation of the New Era, the emancipated God. In you lies the fulfillment of Christ and his Shadow; both the Light and the Dark unite in you. You are Aquarius incarnate."

"But, I'm an old man already."

"It can only happen to an older man in the second half of life. Are you willing to suffer the pain of recognition and the ultimate acceptance?"

"If this constitutes my wholeness, or leads to it, yes, I am willing."

"Good. Close your eyes and listen."

The moment I close my eyes a fierce negative reaction sets in. I am livid, furious and feel terribly insulted by that anima. Such utter foolishness I have never written before or heard. I pace the floor, unwilling to continue. Oh, how I hate to be made a fool. What shall I do?

It is an hour later, and I am back at my window. A cup of coffee and a talk with my wife have calmed me. My unconscious recognizes my resistance and better be wiser with me. I will try to continue and see what has to rise up still from the nether world.

"Through the ages the goal of life's quest has been achieved mainly through the will and the ability to conquer. There has been much misuse of the sword. The true 'way' lies, this time, not through conquest but sooner through acquiescence, as in the symbol of the soft, penetrating wind. The wind and the sun, both natural elements, are needed to bring about the greater consciousness of the New Age. Their penetration is slow, gradual and agonizing. There will be many surprises for you in this new attitude and many new realizations.

"Now be quiet, be calm. Do you know what that is? Calm down, rest, open yourself to the wind as it comes to you now.

Be like a lamb of God, be unprotected – the Nothingness of Being – and fill yourself with the emptiness of the World Soul. Then, listen to the whispering winds. What do they say to you? 'You are God, you are the Right and the Left hand of God. You are All that is – and the Nothingness is the Fullness of the All.'

"Now listen again – and what does the Lion say? 'Thou art King and Prince of Man.' Now listen, oh Erlo, listen to the Nothingness of All Being and in that place lie down to hear a message unable to be received while standing. 'You are the Channel,' it says – and the message roars through your Void.

"You are the Channel of God's Aquarius. There is nothing to accept. There is nothing to believe – only the knowledge of your Void which tells, 'You are the Channel of God.' Now don't get up and don't move, lest your knowledge is not fully anchored. Don't cry – don't stir. Stay the Void and the Channel.

"Your eyes are closed. You are listening. You know – now say, 'I am the Channel, I am God, I am Erlo, I am the Void – the Nothing and the All.'

"Now, as you are through with me and have experienced what you are, go to your wife and with her accept the verities of the Void and know, once and for all, that you are what I said. Say to yourself, 'I am the Channel, I am the God and the Void, Aquarius I am – and Erlo.'"

A wave of emotion sweeps over me as I see the past and the present. I am drowning in tears for what, oh what, will be the future? I know I am a channel; I know what it is to be the Lamb of God. May God's grace be with me as I re-enter my personal being – my poor uneducated self – my flesh – my personality, which will have to carry all this immenseness. Yes, I know I am Aquarius – Erlo. But how that realization will affect my wife and myself, I don't know.

The call of Isaiah now rises up from within me. "Whom shall I send and who will go for us," God asks. And Isaiah rushing forward says, "Here am I. Send me."

How different it is with me now. I don't move. I abide my time. I let the wind move me – let the Universal Spirit touch me and penetrate my Being. But, oh Lord, let me, Erlo, live as I am – as you have created me in your image.

Like the *prima materia* I feel – am unformed being opposite the overwhelming spirit of the Cosmos. I am really what I always was and will be – my self – a riddle, with the capacity for fear and trepidation but also for peace and courage to face the future. Who or whatever I may be, oh Lord, grant me your grace in the future as you did in the past. I know I am a teacher among men, and I know men teach me.

The storm is clearing. All afternoon we had torrential rains, and in the Engadine it is terribly cold.

August 17, 1966
Sils Maria

My dear Mother Goddess, it seems I have to talk to you this morning. Before I can continue any further, I have to contact my own deepest level, the root from which my Christian ancestors sprang. There are three characters, in particular, with whom I have to deal. I truly loathe to meet them again. I call them always my archetypal ancestors. How I wish I could stay impersonal towards them, but they are too alive in me. In fact, the ancestor who is truly the root of my being once threatened me with a terrible oath if I would not recognize him as a vital aspect of myself. I hate even to tell you their names and if I did not see them approach me now through a heavy fog, I would not try to bother with them. But here they are, all three; the Princely Priests or Prophets and the King himself. Mother Goddess, their names, are Isha Jahu (Isaiah), his successor Alfrenennon, known as Isaiah II – the author of the Ugly Servant – and in between these illustrious men is the King, Antiochus III, known as the Great.

I see the Mother Goddess now. Stately she stands, her penetrating gaze clarifying the three figures so that they are fully visible and bathed in the total light of her consciousness. The Mother Goddess is touched.

"They are three glorious characters and they exist in you, my dear Erlo. If only my humanity could realize its ancestral roots," and saying these words she stretches out her arms to embrace the men silently. To my astonishment, the Mother Goddess looks pained. She turns away, and while her eyes take on that hard, cold stare of a Goddess, she murmurs most humanly, "Oh my sons, my sons, what sacrifices you made." Thinking in aeons, she remembers the terrible difficulties of the past and wonders what the New God will bring to her Earth. In sudden desperation she shrieks, "Lord, why do you sacrifice my sons? Is their greatness too much for you?"

No answer came from the Heavens to which she addressed herself. But from the woods behind the mist comes the voice of young Aquarius, gentle and full of respect, saying: "Mother Goddess, I promise in my reign I will not sacrifice your sons. Their death will be according to a different law, perhaps more human. Remember, oh Mother Goddess, that the Christ is resurrected in me. My shadow and his shadow are one. Thus the Word can become flesh in greater measure. Man's shadow, when accepted, creates greater tolerance."

The Wise Mother of All recognizes the voice. She hears in it the compassion and love for mankind and these feelings totally overwhelm her. Unable to stand, she sinks down onto her rock, sobbing for her martyrs, her daughters and her sons. This is her moment of great grief through which she enters the aeon of Aquarius. The new ruler has made her more than divine. Now, she is a woman. Her name is Sophia.

At this moment, my five Christian pilgrims, Asterius, Judas Barsabas, Wilfred, Walter de Gray and François Fénelon appear sitting together on a semi-circled stone bench. Unknown to me, they had witnessed the entire drama of the encounter of the Great Mother with their archaic ancestors and the miracle of her humanization. They are entranced at the immediacy of the prophets and the King, for they understand so well that the existence of these men had affected their own lives deeply. Then a distressing thought wells up within me. How difficult it will be to live through the next development; the coming together of the God-woman with the Christian bishops, the prophets and the King. And where am I, Erlo, in all this? That question, I feel, must solve itself through a rhythm inherent in life.

Sophia, the Great Lady, seats herself among my forebears in the middle of the bench. Aquarius, unseen, watches from a vantage point. There is no escape. Life and its rhythm go on; it builds and it builds. But how I would like to stop the flow, for now I am entering the pre-Christian aeon of the Ram. How much further my Lord, how much further do I have to go? Nevertheless the bridge into the past is being built; it is the will and the need of Aquarius. Thus, I am confronted with Antiochus.

This great warrior spirit and conqueror of the Near and Far East comes towards me, kneels and displays his magnificent fiery sword. Then, with a sudden thrust, he plunges it into the soil. At the sight of this nuptial union, a quiver goes through me. Upon the withdrawal of the sword, I see the last drop of dark red blood drip from the tip and the cleansed weapon, symbol of Antiochus' power and might, is put ceremoniously into my lap.

At that instance fatigue comes over me. There is an unwillingness to continue to experience the magic of these symbolic encounters any longer. A real fear touches me for the moment. However, in total disregard of my reactions, Antiochus the Great stands up, swings his golden mantle around me, places his circlet on my head, and kneels, again. I know he wants to say something, but I don't want to listen. His eyes fix themselves upon me and our souls meet. No withdrawal is possible now. "Forgive me, Antiochus," I say. "I want to prevent your talking. The mantle – the sword – the crown are unaccustomed fearful burdens."

With deep feeling, humility and respect, Antiochus answers me: "Don't identify, Erlo, with these symbols. Just let, for a moment, the burdens they represent sink deep into your heart. Then you will be freed from them. I carried these encumbrances for you with total identification, until the beautiful love of a true woman released me from the bond with my Kingship. Now my crown rests upon your head, my mantle upon your shoulders. All is of pure gold as it should be, for my old rule has come to its end. My power and my glory are yours, and so is my worldly kingdom. Deep within me, in my most royal self, I grant you the treasures of my world. Take my sword in your right hand, the one which holds your pen." I do so. "Now, present this sword to the Heavens and swear that it will be drawn only to the glory of Heaven and Earth, and so create greater awareness."

As I hold the sword up, the heavens open and send a bolt of lightning to its tip. The electrical charge travels into my arm and brings such energy that my body shakes from the impact. The sword extends itself into one side of an ellipse, which soon straightens out.

Then my inner voice speaks up: "With this sword I will destroy and resurrect. It extends into the Heavens – it penetrates into the Earth. It is powerful, willful, strong in steel and texture. It is mine – it is God's."

Antiochus hears everything and is at rest. Lady Sophia, realizing danger in the timidity of my outer being, leaves her place among my Christian ancestors and strides towards me. She takes the sword, handles it lustily in circular movements and returns it saying: "Take it – don't cringe! Slay with it! Use it! Don't fail it! It is power and strength; it is wisdom and energy. Handle it wisely, but never fail to use it for if you can't destroy, you can't create. A man has a sword; if it is not used, he loses himself in me. It belongs to his conscious power as well as to the Logos. Nothing can develop unless it is wielded properly. No plowshare is possible until the power of the sword of righteousness is established, nor can there be peace unless the sword protects it. The sword is male. Girdle it, have it ready at hand. It is to be used against civilization's decadence and the weakening of man's instinctive vitality. Use it to divide the chaff from the wheat, right from wrong. It shall be a tool of awareness – and spermatic power."

After these words, the Mother Goddess places Antiochus at my left shoulder as a sentinel to watch over the peculiar, paradoxical acts of the sword. Antiochus, while taking his place, prays to himself: "Power, oh glorious power, beware of your shadow." This prayer makes the mother Sophia turn around on the way back to the bench and issue a warning: "Once you relax and let your sword be taken from you, you hand its power over to ignorance and slime."

I watch Her Majesty Sophia seat herself among my colorful ancestors. With the luminous woods behind them, the King at my side and the great prophets nearing me, my heart starts to beat wildly. I can't manage this vision any longer. I shout, "Lord help me – I won't be faced now with another encounter." Typical twentieth century rationalism takes hold of me and I tear myself out of the inner world of realities. I have to halt.

How fearful I am. The differences between the inner and outer world rile me in a terrible way. I know it is I who live in rebellion, and I am shocked and rocked to the bottom of my personality. The negating of my ordinary, everyday, civilized living by these archaic characters is just hell on me. I would love to challenge not only Isaiah, but also the world for printing, preaching, and reprinting prophesies that were, at times, incorrect. The power of their words and worlds is purely psychic it seems to me at this moment, and I don't want to get trapped in a reality beyond the grasp of my present, rebellious, conscious mind. Oh, how I would love to withdraw and forever swear off my great ancestors; to find fault with their existences. But now my recalcitrant rationalism will have to be quiet, for all of a sudden, in the midst of this fury, my vision breaks open again.

There they are, the two Isaiahs, the two martyr prophets. They had the unbelievable courage to live a life of total devotion to their God, which is the very thing I am not willing to do now. I am seated again; Antiochus is there, my ancestors, the Anima Mundi and the Isaiahs. Isaiah the elder nears me. Automatically I rise, for his presence imbues me with warmth and respect. Our eyes meet on a level, and I can feel his thoughts and hear his words.

"I was full of divine fire and I was quoted and requoted and listened to and it was right, for my words inspired the people as they had inspired me. They are still not wrong but you, Erlo, do not want to be burned by the divine word. Once you heard Kerel tell you – I know it is years ago but I will make you listen again – 'It is not what you say, it is from where you say it.' What I said and wrote was burned into me, and I spoke with sacerdotal fire. Right or wrong, those words carry their magic. Criticize them, fear them, evaluate them with your present day consciousness, but know where my words still have value and where they fail you."

Then the mighty man stepped aside and Isaiah the second took his place next to the forefather. "Two hundred years later I lived. Pain inspired me and fright brought me to my innermost writing. Life dictated; I recorded as well as I could. There is neither praise nor blame in what I did."

The atmosphere is charged with emotion. The Christians look intent and are horrified at my attitude, which wants to scrutinize the prophets' Divine Messages. I look at the Isaiahs – so simple – so direct they are. Then the reaction sets in. My knees feel weak. I cannot stand up or speak. I sit down, look aside and feel a last, strong, wicked viper rise up in me. "I know there is plenty of the cynic in me, my dear ancestors. I refuse to go that way. I realize fully your powers, but I hate to write or speak in exhortations and ecstasy. I do know that I cannot live without the Divine Word, but I also know that God cannot live here on earth without me. So, I am willing to live in partnership with God having the majority shares, but I have the rights of the minority. I will fight for those rights, which are the rights of the individual. I know you both represent the voice of God to the world; to me you don't. Part of what you wrote I still consider to be obscure and passé, but let me end our meeting now for I have to walk and rest and then I will be willing to face you again."

August 17, 1966
Late afternoon

I walked through the beautiful larch woods behind the hotel this late afternoon alone and bitter. The impact of the morning was so severe. Why are the ancestors after me? I thought. But, as usual, a meditative rest enters me when I meander on the paths here. I look over the meadows below and see the happy vacationers enjoying the Engadine lakes and mountains. I sit down thinking of all my experiences of the morning, not knowing if I would really like to meet the prophets again. It was all decided for me though, as a strange thing happened.

While leaning against a tree I felt as if my clothes were not my own, and instead of my sweater and sports attire I was dressed in ancient Egyptian costume. It was Isaiah the Second, the evangelical prophet, who in full splendor of his court dress took possession of me. Afrenennon or Alfrenennon is his name.

"I want you to know, dear Erlo, that this is the way I looked when I fled Egypt and became an exile. Later, I will tell you much more about myself. In your life I stand for the very opposite of Antiochus. If you compare him with the Logos, I am the one who carries the Eros. You fight me and fight me at every possible turn, for whenever I make myself felt, you suffer. But through that suffering you can digest and understand your life with greater clarity. As all was taken from me of worldly splendors and I experienced one debacle after another, I became the man of sorrow. That sorrow was not the sorrow of sack and ashes, but the deep Light-giving sorrow which creates wisdom.

"Through the pain and agony of my God-given soul I wrote and created," Alfrenennon continues. "That was my road to 'Comfort ye – Comfort ye.' The splendor of life was revealed through the agonies of my suffering, the shadows being so black, so disastrous and inhuman that the only road to my salvation was the Light and Love of God. The intense everlasting interest and support of all that is living belongs to the Eros – even the smallest movement of the arm or finger is observed by the Eros side of God. We, as humans, supply the warmth from the hearth of our heart to this Divine Principle, so that in the darkest places we can bring comfort. This is what I lived and experienced. This is my gift to you, this is what my life was about, and this is what I gave to the world."

I walked back to the hotel repeating and repeating his words. I remembered the feelings of a deep, intense, powerful breathing and a rhythm of eternal well-being which came when he spoke. Now, while seated again at my window in my room I still have a silence in me which comes with the acceptance of "Comfort ye – Comfort ye." My beautiful evangelical friend seems to rest in my heart; if only I could stay with that feeling. But, in our civilization, bells ring which call us back to other realities. Dinner bells, telephone bells – and the ear is already cocked for an interruption so that the mood lasts only a short moment. It is the twentieth century and although this age is connected with other centuries, hurry and pressure are most disastrously interfering with our native rhythms. So I stare out of the window, calm, relaxed but on the alert at the same time.

It is late in the day now and our last night here in Sils Maria will be quickly upon us. We love this place and we will leave with many happy memories about our walks in the Vex Thal and on the mountain slopes full of wildflowers. Ann has been painting on an enormous long scroll. It is a creation myth in color. When I write she paints, and our room functions well. The prophets and ancestors are at home here with us. This has been a terrific day and I am not through yet, for the mighty

Isaiah seems still to have a message and I will respond most likely with my comment.

I close my eyes and right away I am back again with the ancestor. "Hear ye, Erlo, hear ye my beloved son," says Isaiah, almost drowning me with his presence. The tone is like a call to arms of Isaiah the Mighty – tree, trunk and root of my life. "I have watched you and tried to lead you many times. My words have guided your Christian ancestors around many difficult corners and obstacles, but when I come in touch with you I know I have to deal with a different spirit. The Aquarian stands right behind you – recalcitrant – and still intensely interested in the great past. You fear my spirit, Erlo, and so does Aquarius for deep within you say, 'Can this old man still be of use to us?'

"Yes, I can. Never cut down your ancestral tree for its spirit will be lost and you will be rootless. Prune, trim but don't kill, for the juices of life run through our roots to the fruit. I am your tree, your spiritual ancestor. Although we all work for the fruit of life, that does not mean it always contains our essence; neither is the fruit our greatest value. The moments I am One with God, the moments I suffer his total nearness, is the great value of my existence. This directness, this Oneness with the World Soul containing all there is in this world, is the beauty and grandeur of my life. Each time this contact happens words flow from me like a rushing stream. This spirit of being One with All is of my essence.

"I answered the call of God who was looking for a warm, loving, vigorous soul to take on a special task. Only God knows this task in its fullness. When I heard that call, cosmic energies rushed through me like a great wind and I answered, 'Here I am, oh Lord.' Completely overwhelmed by my own essence, I answered for all time and surrendered in total devotion to his will.

"With full vigor and lust for life I went about my task. I don't know that much about Logos or Eros. The universe is One, undivided full glory to me; God and I as One word, God and I united in action. And that union is manifest in my writing.

That union is my spirit as well as yours and is not only my gift to you, but God's gift to you also."

Then Isaiah, my Isha, steps forward to kiss me on the forehead. The immense vitality of this beautiful figure, this towering eminence, forces me to embrace him. I hug him hard against me as if to absorb his undaunted power.

Looking at all my soulmates I am deeply moved and feel the need to declare my own place with them. Isaiah, ancestor of all that is mine, I love you for your outpouring of vital life force. It refreshes me; it puts me deep into myself. You lived and wrote in your time with such intensity that not only did you reach your own center, but also the center of many after you. I will do my best, more than my best even, to enter my own spirit in my own way and so perhaps reach the spirit of those around me. Endless and tortuous seems the road to me, for the call of the Lord as Aquarius must be as complicated and far-reaching as the call you had to live. As life touches me, so I will respond hopefully to the deepest level. I will not write for humanity but only for my own human need and experience.

Your gifts of today, my dear ancestors, have overwhelmed me and made me aware of my smallness and stubbornness. I will give in, I promise, for my own sake, otherwise I know I will become totally unadjusted. You are part of me; you are my mystery, my past. My future will be decided by what I have lived through you. Aquarius, don't hide anymore; come out of the woods. I am ready. I am willing to stand in your Light. The Mother Goddess; my ancestors; we are all with you. Reveal yourself now and teach me as we will teach you.

I hear the village church bells. It is midnight; a new day is dawning. I am on my way back into the world. Ragaz and Sils Maria have been witness to my inner realities. Tomorrow, my wife and I are going to Holland and, after a short stay there, we will leave for America. We are now on the path, on the road to my homeland – America.

August 24, 1966
Voorschoten, Holland

At my family's

"Good God, where are you? I've been looking and looking for you. You've stayed away so long. I told you, an the Anima Mundi told you, you cannot do this to me. This is Aquarius speaking. We need a *plan de campagne*. You can't push me into the corner just for family reasons. Travel is one thing, but family gossip is something altogether different. We are all in need of our scribe, and your welfare as well as ours depends on our working together. There will be no rest for you, nor will you feel anchored unless you keep our daily contact going. The Mother Goddess is often cool and removed, but I, Aquarius, need and want my daily exercise with you. I'm a spirit, the new spirit, but remember I am a very definite entity in you. In your writing I was born the moment Christ united with his Shadow. Christ and his Shadow are in me. Christ and Lucifer, the Right hand and the Left hand of God, are no longer Fishes of black and gold. Instead they are my hands, God's hands, and yours.

"Now I know about your bitterness at times, your recalcitrant ways of going about life. I know your immeasurable fear for the darkness of God, for the deep, black suffering of the incomprehensible. I have seen your record. I saw your lives registered, one after the other, and witnessed their immense efforts to live up to Christ's teachings. I saw your dismay and despising of the Dark brother. I saw your fear, as well as God's fear, expressed in the Lord's Prayer at his Last Supper: 'Give us this day our daily bread, and lead us not into temptation, but deliver us from evil.' I am aware of the entire horror of Yahweh, the cruel notions of men's mind and God's mind belonging also to God's ego, the entire misery and fear of human existence echoed in the prayers of the Lord Christ.

"And how right, how right, for the aeon of the Fishes had one terrifying omission. The one I refer to is the terror of blackness not being dealt with, so that through our denial of God's dark side blackness could not be redeemed. The redeemer was the Christ, the Prince of Peace and Light, but where was the redeemer of our Deepest Darkness? Surely he was not sufficiently represented by the one-sidedness of the Christ symbol, a symbol that did not relate to or want to contact the darkness of God. In opposite directions the Fishes swam, and so the Left hand of God was left out, left alone. The *manus sinistra* stayed black and unredeemed – Lucifer functioning more as the Devil than as the Light Bearer. Thank God for the many heretical sects and individuals who sacrificed themselves to carry the Light in Darkness. Through the ages they held an archaic principle alive, and hope for the human race was not lost. Now comes my reign, and with my reign my influence upon more comprehensive living.

"A beautiful, powerful dream was given to you, my dear Erlo (you dreamed it for all of us), in which my strength, my basic instinctive energies show themselves to be equal to my task. In your dream, the Princes of Darkness and of Light, Lucifer and Christ, like a wind, are both equally dealt with – each in their own way. The Christ knows that he has in me, Aquarius, a powerful ally. Remember how I withstood a fierce onslaught of Lucifer, the Black Fish? The sinister hand of God brought his Light to me, as I got to know him through a fight from sunset to sunrise. With that dawn I felt my strength and knew that in my reign my spirit can redeem the dark blackness of human suffering. Christ entered you, Erlo, a most human form, and shook hands with me and so the union took place of the Light of Day and the Light of Night and it was one circle without end. Sun or no sun, moon or no moon, I encompassed the cycle of the Shadow and the Light.

"This you know, Erlo, is the truth which was brought to you many years ago in a dream, only half comprehended then. But let me refresh your memory. That dream started in a cave in which you found yourself with the Earth Mother. She pointed to a lectern on which was spread a large map of your native land that showed the East and the West divided by a large body of water. Then she said unto you, 'Bring East and West together, and when you are able to solve how that is to be done, great riches will become available to you and all those capable of making that union.' I tell you now, dear Erlo, uniting the two was really well-nigh an impossibility during the last aeon. The split, the difference between East and West was too great, the waters were too deep, and the cosmic forces themselves were working in fierce opposition.

"Then, as you were looking at the map and wondering how such a thing would ever be possible, it was shown to you how I, Aquarius, the ruling God of the New Dawn, survived and lived through this problem. In the continuation of your dream lies the answer.

"Pondering over the map, the great Dark Messenger was sent to you. He was sent by the Christ, as he told you. He bowed deeply to you and you did likewise, realizing his importance. Not until now, today, did you know that this Dark God was looking at you not any more as a victim of his evil will, but rather he looked at you as the very subject of his own redemption. All night long, as you remember, that dark horrifying power of the Lord's might had been fighting with me. My fight was a night fight, a terrible battle of changing times, in which the New Aeon was realizing the fact that Darkness could not conquer or stay separate anymore and is part of all creation.

"For in this fight I got to know every trick, every movement of the Dark and never did I try to kill it. I, Aquarius, am not out for murder, or for despising. In fighting, my love rose, my love became a flame and with that flame I touched the Darkness and met the heart of Lucifer – and we knew we were one and the same. Then, with a roar of agony the Black Messenger sank to his knees. And so did I. We prayed for understanding, and as I rose full of love for my Dark Opponent, he thundered: 'Redeem me, be my guiding light, for deep in the Darkness I carry your Light. We are one. Don't separate me anymore.'

"This all occurred while you, Erlo, were in the cave with the Earth Mother showing you, on the map, the split between East and West which she wanted you to integrate. Then the Dark One heard the call of the Christ, who said to him, 'Fetch me the man in whose heart and mind I cried for wholeness.' You were brought out of the cave into the meadow, the green grasses, where you turned to the left. Not finding anyone, you retraced your steps and went straight forward, bearing slightly to the right. You went along the stone wall that was beside your path, and halting at a breach in the wall, Christ, like a wind, rushed into your ears and you were totally possessed by him. Battle weary, I passed you, the possessed one. Then the old King Christ in you, in a way that was simple but so wise, so deeply grateful, called me. And I, looking back and into your eyes saw only the Christ, who extended his hand to me and I put mine in his. That clasp of hands was a moment of triumph.

"I know now you alone were aware that the new, the old and the present met in the warmth of your human hand. I only saw the Christ in your eyes, not aware that you, Erlo, also were there. But the Christ came to meet me, as his Light and prayers for wholeness had caused me to see the Light in my Black Brother. I touched flesh, warm from blood. I shook and shuddered for it was my first contact with the human being, and I walked away on the path towards the left into the unconscious of man. Then, I did not know the importance of touching the human through the guiding Christ principle. I could only think of the battle I had with my Dark side, my own Blackness, and that I had come out of it unscathed. The Christ had crowned that terrific battle by entering and possessing a warmblooded body so that I could feel it and come to know that all meets in the human hand. This contact with you was bewildering magic. I know now that I have found the Light of Darkness, and so in all mankind this principle is kindled through our handshake brought about by the love of Christ for humanity.

"And you, Erlo, in deep silence, you turned towards your path of further development protected by Jupiter, Father of all. I turned around to look at you and saw him on your right in his full regalia. On the Dark Continent of Africa he is called the Morning Star; primordial man called him the Heart of Dawn.

"I have touched you through Christ and now I know my way into you. Let me shake hands with you again, my dear Erlo. Look into my eyes and there will be peace in you and strength and fulfillment."

I do, and his eyes are happy and laughing – but I am tired. I stop now.

August 25, 1966
Voorschoten, Holland

The Prophecy of Aquarius

I have just come upstairs, after leaving my family, to go to the guest room to write.

> "I, Aquarius, am the Great Awakener, the Great Strengthener of all faith. Through me, the doors open into the Hereafter. For me, all worlds will melt into One. The Oneness of All will be the message. The Divine and Subdivine, the Upper and Lower worlds will find their bridge so that All will be as One undivided world with its different parts interrelated and entwined. Such power will be to my words that kingdoms will disappear and appear in fast and constant change. Flux and change will be so that nothing will harden into form until the time is ripe and the knowledge such that changes are to be known as forms of life, like the winds coming from constantly changing corners."

I will join my sisters now, for the usual late cup of tea. The last part of the prophecy sounds like the Book of Changes, the *I Ching* with its sixty-four major situations of life.

August 29, 1966
M.S. Princess Margriet

On the ocean. Very windy; heavy waves.

"Erlo, my dear man, I am not going to stand around corners just waiting for you to start writing. There has to be a time set aside for it."

"There is no easy formula Aqui, especially on the ocean."

"Try to work in the morning, Erlo."

"My heart starts to beat too fast when you say that. Also, my system is upset."

"This afternoon you had dreams telling you about hoodlums, and they, you are aware, represent your negative side. You are fighting me, and that is what you get."

"That is right. One dream was also about a green child, a small magical figure. I suppose that figure belongs to you. What really frightens me is your forcing me into contact with unknown worlds and strange realities."

"That is not correct, Erlo; you are hiding and hope in this way to escape close contact with me. The moment you are near to me you will feel better. Now think about that!"

"I feel you are right Aqui, but strong powers have to come into action to overcome my instinctive rebellion and reluctance."

September 3, 1966
Saturday on the Ocean

Princess Margriet

Out of the sea this morning arose a woman – a Dark Woman – with golden strands in her hair. With an imperious gesture of her arm she pointed towards me. Her voice roared like the ocean waves and echoed in my head. This is what she said:

"O dark one – and more than dark in my eyes – your rebellion and reluctance, your ignorance on which you even pride yourself, is appalling. Don't you recognize that you share in the great drama of this glorious age? A unique burden rests upon your shoulders. Remember my showing you the map of your native land and explaining to you about the immense riches becoming available to all who can unite the opposites of East and West? East is Aquarius, West is Christ. East is the Heart of Dawn, West is the Love of Life. Endless are those opposites, but your task is the union of the two divine manifestations of the changing aeon – Christ and Aquarius. Imbue yourself, lose yourself; there is no choice. Christ was and is; Aquarius is and will be. Aquarius has the power to carry both Light and Dark; that was the message of your dream. His road is the road of Christ and his Shadow. The development of the aeon to come is now revealed to you. All of humanity's suffering of the last aeon is to be redeemed, purified and understood as well as can be done by my children.

"And you, my son, beholder of the precious jewel of the uniting of the Great Stars of past and present, you have been shown the unconquerable power of Aquarius over the darkest shadow of the antichrist. In your hands in the dream, my precious gift, lies the knowledge of a conquering hero; a capacity in your soul, in God, in me – Goddess of all – to relate the opposites to each other and to shake hands. Carry then, my son, this magnificent fact to a waiting world and don't tarry with your reluctances. Now, before entering New York City, realize this ability and carry its knowledge in the cave of your heart where you saw me, and from where I teach you. This power to unite the opposites is also the reason why the Buddha visited you at your bedside, and asked for your precious semen to be sprayed upon his chest in the form of a peacock's tail."

A tremor ran all through me, and I answered proudly, but so timidly: "Yes, Mother of my Heart, Cave of Darkness, Mate, Goddess and even sometimes Wife of my dreams – I know you are right. I know I am living out an archetype again. Once more there is an Antiochus or an Isaiah in me. I see this morning, while writing in my book, the story of a mighty spirit and its many lives living a part of the Great Design through the ages. The same spirit has grown richer and greater through the transitions of time. Again, I am following the God of the aeon. This time the individual, Erlo, although immersed in the Great Drama, looks on and tries to obey and comprehend. I know that life is greater than I am and many are the powers I cannot grasp. I accept my fate now – not without tears. I accept it with love, as I sense the closeness of your Being. I will follow my life's design and do my utmost to swim with it. I am now on my way as an Aquarian."

September 5, 1966
On the ocean, along the American coast

Princess Margriet

"I, Aquarius, await you. Through centuries you have been preparing yourself to become a true Aquarian teacher. It was under my auspices that your soul descended to Earth for the first time as Isaiah. I, the Aquarian, was in full charge of his approach to life. Isaiah was my delight because his power was so vital, so undisturbed by the experiences of former earthly lives. Now, alas, your soul, following the Wheel of Life, is living under the auspices of Virgo so that you, Erlo, look at me with a critical eye, evaluating, trying to bring clarity where I prefer Darkness to reign. But Erlo refuses Darkness without Light, and I am forced, constantly forced, to become aware of things which my nature wants to continue just as before, unclarified, without the eyes of a twentieth century upstart like you. I am much more ancient than your soul ever could be. Why can't I be what I always have been, a tremendous, eternal power – without bothering about consciousness?

"You upstarts are bending my will, a divine will, and you allow and don't allow; you criticize and you bend me towards a realization of who and what you are. Your powerful human minds put searchlights into my deep darkness like darts into my soul. Who wants that! I want to reign supreme and unhindered by awareness. I saw the mighty Christ bow down and pray for his wholeness. It filled me with utmost holiness, and you defiled him, you filthy human. In his name you committed crime upon crime. What do you intend to do to me with your foul, limiting brain? Are you divinely gifted as to play havoc with your gods and shape them to your liking? Curses a thousandfold on your head if ever you dare to twist me and to crumple me like a piece of paper, to declare me passé one day!"

Through my porthole I see dark clouds gathering together and I expect a furious Aquarius to throw a thunderbolt any moment. After that tongue-lashing I feel, most curiously, a love rising for the new god, a deep compassion for his life task, and so I hear myself answer:

"Aquarius, dearest Aquarius, in coming to your throne on this Earth you start to taste the difficulties of incarnation. Your descent out of the Heavens is hard and holds all the sorrows of our human lives. Even you are but the servant of God, as I am. You and I have to fight our battles and, as now, each other. Through these fights, like Arjuna, you will receive your earthly education. Mighty spirit that you are you must know, like all gods, that a fallibility exists in you which you will have to experience and through which painful wisdom will flower in your divine but youthful mind. Your reign follows the rule of Christ as lived by us humans. He was in bondage like you are now. To me, this mighty bondage of man to his God is all there is of importance. Through this tie a direct contact is created so that my consciousness can bring its tribute to the great Source, the great Dynamo of Love and Power. You, my dearest Aquarius, are in bondage to me, a human. Through love of this Earth you are inexorably entwined with all of us. We will have to dance the rhythms of Death and Life, Birth and Rebirth.

"Kick! Scream! Shout to the heavens! Do what you have to in your agony of becoming tied to me. All I can say is that I could no more escape our marriage than you, and I have learned through bitter, bitter tears that I love life and so I love you, too. This is very hard to say for I know you will be a difficult taskmaster, and I will rebel. Understand, for my sake, that you will have to bring me again and again to the place where I will be able to accept you and, I hope, comprehend you – as far as that is possible. Of course, I will misinterpret you and you will change, the way any archetype goes through its changes and learns. Life will provide many curious twists and circumstances. More often than not, they will be hard to understand or to believe that they are brought about by the Divine Will. But one thing we will know; you will learn and so will I, and no true consciousness will be lost. All of it will be stored and gathered in the Heart of the Lord, far beyond the reach of Time and there, in deep contemplation, this Heart of God – the Lord Matreya – will breathe of his own substance, which is yours, Aquarius, and mine. The great realization will take place beyond our comprehension, but totally dependent upon us, the living eyes of God. At the end of your reign we will look at each other in the mirror of Time, and the waters of your jug will spill over into Capricorn."

Aquarius listens to me, and off he walks to contemplate this intuitive wisdom, aware that his rebellion has brought him fruit. Human contact is a bewildering and painful experience, he thinks. The words, "end of reign, mirror of Time" irritate him, but in some miraculous way keep reverberating in his mind. They carry a truth which he has known for aeons, but of which he was previously unaware. So, there he goes, the great Aquarius. This contact is the beginning, the first rebellion put straight.

"Damn those humans! Damn them especially when they say things you really know are true but would like to overthrow. Damn those laws which rule both god and man! There is no escape. And what is worse, within that kind of wisdom my power is undone." Then Aquarius thinks of the Christ, the

Great Fisherman, and he realizes how his spirit must have suffered. Instinctively, he senses now the pain of earthly living; he senses how humanity lived that unavoidable split between body and soul under Christ's rule. "What will be my cross," he asks – "And where is it? Will the world be able to meet the challenge of my reign in any better way? Oh Lord, my God, where is your love for me? Will I succeed? Will I be able to pass on my love for You and creation any better than Christ? I will walk among men, with Christ on my right and the Dark Brother on my left."

Further and further Aquarius walks into his green psychic landscape, wondering what will happen when he meets the Christ. All of a sudden he sees Christ, somewhat tired, sitting on his rock, called by some the "philosopher's stone." It is full of inscriptions put there since time immemorial.

Christ, personification of the entire era of Pisces, looks at his young successor with all the love and wisdom gathered in the last two thousand years. Tears well up when he speaks gently to Aquarius. "Humanity, with its chaotic, quixotic mind will give your spirit a thousand and one interpretations. You will be more easily understood than I, however. My spirit is so much like the Fishes, swimming to and from in opposite directions. Neither direction is right without the experience and knowledge of the other. But so few, so few were strong enough to stand the tension of such powerful opposites. Not until the end of my time did I become aware of my own duality. At the crucifixion came my total union with God the Father. All was Spirit and Light. From this union the divine spark was released so that each individual could claim his own divinity. And from Golgotha, the power of this accomplishment, this realization on Earth of individual divinity, spread and is still the root of your tree, my dear Aquarius.

"Spirit and Light were supreme and, drunk with this realization, Jesus of Nazareth sent the Devil away. This banishment was not naive however; it was in the spirit of the time, in the nature of humanity and its fate which allows only a narrow passage to the full truth. Not until much later would the Dark aspect, the other Fish, have power enough to make its imprint. For its full redemption we have awaited your coming. It was a long, long, wait. The descent of God in me with its outpouring of the Holy Ghost started to work in the minds of men. Then, in order to make this spirit available to mankind, a religion was formed. Thus was created a church, a dogma – a set form with its inevitable danger of sterility. My spirit would have died had it not been for the remnant of valiant souls keeping me alive in their hearts and seeing me and looking for me in the thousands of ways and processes God has created for us all in his image. And this is the way it will be with your spirit, Aquarius. Forms will be created and overthrown; your real spirit, never fear, will always come through in inspired individuals in spite of all rules and regulations. There is nothing wrong in that." Turning deeper into himself, Christ continues in a whisper: "Earthly life is very painful. The pain of sorrow, the tears of death – these are the flowers of wisdom, the blossoming of the Self."

Aquarius looks away from Christ and sees the long, long road ahead of him. But the Christ, still turned inwardly, suddenly cries out with joy: "Look back, Aquarius! Look back to the idea, the very source of my conception." And young Aquarius, who really loves to look back, looks and looks and cannot believe his eyes or his ears – for there, from way back, he sees the strong immense Isaiah waving and smiling and a host of angels and spirits comes with him. Now Christ tells Aquarius: "Look further back into time, seven hundred years before my birth, when Isaiah stood at the 'conduit of the upper pool' in Jerusalem. There, in his extreme frustration with the sly King Ahaz, he realized, from the very bottom of his soul, the future manifestation of Emmanuel (God within us), Savior and Redeemer. You, Aquarius, are the new Emmanuel. God is with you in his new form. Isaiah received the message of divine intent two thousand six hundred years ago, and his spirit is coming to your help. Isaiah is still very alive in the thoughts of man and is your root as well as mine."

September 8, 1966
New York City

Aquarius waits to see the strange host of spirits as they come nearer. He trembles slightly in apprehension. They look biblical, antiquated and his vital young spirit is antagonistic towards the old man. They have had their time; why keep those damn everlasting ideas so alive, he thinks. Let them lay undisturbed in their own past and not come to mingle in his affairs. Christ reads Aquarius' thoughts, but makes no answer to this youthful foolishness. He knows that Isaiah's presence will soon put an end to this willful thinking.

Isaiah comes closer until he stands squarely in front of young Aquarius. Love emanates from him, and smiling broadly he puts out his big strong arms to embrace Aquarius. Isaiah just loves to hug this new power of God's expression. "For twenty-six hundred years my voice has been heard," he says to Aquarius. "That is a long, long time. My admonitions and warnings have made many a timid soul tremble. My faith and trust in the covenant with God has encouraged many strong, brilliant individuals all through the centuries. Through my descendants I have preached and fought for the truth, although sometimes my soul was in agony and doubt when I learned that my descendants would turn to a dogma or a pot of gold, instead of feeding themselves with the riches of the spirit. However, through all of this I became a much wiser man."

Aquarius looks at sturdy Isaiah and thinks him a wonderful apparition; for some perhaps a source of inspirational power but not for his youthful, rebellious mind. So he smiles affably at this engaging relic of mashed-out truth. That prophet is so nice, so theatrical, he muses. Aquarius nods politely and goes on his way, aware only of his own will and strength.

Christ looks on. The situation is awkward. Wasn't this a repetition of what happened at the upper pool outside Jerusalem when King Ahaz artfully evaded the truth? This time Isaiah is blocked not by a King who rules an earthly kingdom, but by Aquarius-Emmanuel who is to rule the psychic kingdom for the next two thousand years. So Christ wonders, what now!

Isaiah watches the departing god and notices the strong shoulders and proud neck of the inexperienced newcomer. He shakes his head and realizes that he has made no impression on Aquarius. Perhaps Isaiah's attitudes are too archaic for the new times; maybe they are not casual or cynical enough.

Christ watches Isaiah and is glad that Aquarius' rebellion arouses the interest of the wise old man. They look at each other and exchange a reassuring smile. Then Isaiah, the undaunted, says: "You rest for a while, I feel this problem is something I have to solve. This young god has to face his ancestor. In your ears, my dear Christ, must still reverberate the death gong of your struggles. Aquarius' star is only just rising into the sun. Who or what can tame the power of the New Age? We don't know. But take your rest, my beloved Emmanuel of former days." Then they kiss in a warm embrace – and Christ comes to rest in Isaiah.

Isaiah, now half-dazed, is wondering what to do. He walks pensively towards the beautifully carved stone where the Christ had been seated just a moment before. Perhaps in this place an inspiration would well up from within him. His compelling eyes, shaded by enormous eyebrows, search around for a solution. He wonders what will happen to his beloved humanity in the hands of this youthful god who is so stubborn, so strong. What if the willful black spirit of immediate power would entice this youngster? Isaiah shudders at the idea of ambitious grabbing for the pot of gold. This shortsighted polluting of man's psyche would make humanity suffer a terrible debacle. Will this new god, this new spirit of Divine Origin, go positive or negative? What is my direction? What is my guiding star? How can I, with my knowledge, help?

Isaiah throws his arms to the Heavens and tears of despair run down his cheek. "Lord," he cries, "our knowledge, our suffering, is it in vain?" Then, a rumble within the stone on which he is sitting echoes thrice in his belly and becomes knowledge as it rises to his head. Isaiah hears the message from the essence of the stone. "Humanity is now given a new form of divine energy. Aquarius, with his two stars of equal magnitude, combines spirit and matter evenly, thus creating a psyche more humane than ever. Heaven and Earth will find greater tolerance and awareness in man, attitudes which will spread infinite blessings. Aquarius will rule. He carries the Waters of Life in a jug on his shoulder and that symbol is his power. The strength he will give to humanity is immense."

Suddenly, a blinding flash of realization comes to Isaiah; the powers of the Godhead will be put into human hands. Now, the Divine energies will flow into each individual, and every man will be able to use or misuse them with renewed strength. Humanity will come of age, and the Divine powers will be invested in man's brain, in his soul, in his psyche, enabling the Aquarian spirit to work more directly with the human race than the spirit of Christ ever could.

"Oh Lord, have mercy! Have mercy for now I, Isaiah, and my descendants will have the difficult task of dealing directly with our Divine powers. We will be like Aquarians, not like Christians. It was through Christ we tried to find our Light; now, it will have to be through Aquarius – and Aquarius is man." Then, remembering that Aquarius' symbol is depicted as a man carrying his own water jug, Isaiah shouts with the greatest joy and relief: "Thank God! Thank God! He carries his own water jug! Thanks to the Lord, he carries his own. Praise be, for he is equipped. Hallelujah! Hallelujah!" In fact, Isaiah makes such a to-do that the host of angels, who usually follow his thoughts as if they are printed words, cannot comprehend him at first, but they see the relief on his face. He smiles and laughs, as if a great burden has fallen away from him. Christ will not have to do it alone at all. The human race is coming of age, and there is the capacity in Aquarius to carry his own.

This realization brings forth an immense joy and the heavens break out in great jubilation with the sounds of Hallelujah. "Aquarius is young, strong, capable! He carries his own portion of the Waters of Life. What maturity this shows; what promise this holds; what opportunities this portends!" sing the angels.

Now, from out of the dark, Isaiah's descendants appear – all of them: François, Walter, Wilfred, Asterius, Judas, Antiochus, and Isaiah II. Solemnly they form a circle, bow their heads and pray an anxious fervent prayer, for they know humanity well and in their hearts they are fearful. Isaiah I breaks into the circle, his mind whirling with these new ideas.[1]

September 11, 1966
Waverstead

As ancestral father to them all, and as adviser to millions, Isaiah I stands thinking. His right hand rises and goes out to Alfrenennon, known to the world as Isaiah II, and his left hand takes hold of François Fénelon. At the same time, all of his descendants close in, forming a tight, magic circle. What a curious lot they are! Like humanity! Incomprehensible! What can he, Isaiah, tell his descendants, each of whom is so different? They have only one thing in common – all are aware that Fate assigned them a role to play in the evolution of humanity. Each of them accepted their role and, to a greater or lesser degree, served humanity in its development. Wouldn't they continue in their roles? What then is so somber in their attitude?

Asterius speaks up: "Isaiah, my dear ancestor, when I welcomed my Christian brothers from Europe, sure in my faith and strong in my trust in Christ, an inexplicable phenomenon occurred in my Church which had nothing to do with my tough, personal experiences. When we gathered

[1] C.G. Jung said: "The world hangs on a thin thread, and that thread is the psyche of man."

before the altar, the altar disappeared, and in its place was only a Hole, a deep, Black Pit. The wailing and the stench that greeted us from that Hole of Darkness was unbearable; the hue and the cry from that Pit of Unlived and Unrealized Life was unbelievable. Yet, above the Pit was a picture of indescribable beauty – the hands of God forming, out of the ether, a ladder to be used to reach all who were buried there since the time of Christ and, who knows, even before that. We are thinking of this Pit, and of Aquarius' youth and inexperience."

At that, a bolt of lightning comes out of the heavens as if it was thrown by the wrath of Jehovah. Thunder is all around. The host of angels flee in holy terror as black clouds gather menacingly from every direction, releasing a torrential rain. The entire atmosphere is filled with primordial power and, in the midst of the terrifying storm, Aquarius appears – calm, unperturbed and fully aware of nature's commotion. An aura of Light surrounds him, and wherever he walks calm and equilibrium are brought about. A god, not a youth walks here. This powerful center of Divine Portent approaches the circle of men, who are already burdened with the inevitable difficulties presented by the release, from the Pit, of unlived, potential life.

"Hear ye, men of Christ and Christian thought. Through me the New Age will find its way, just as inexorably and surely as it has with any other Divine manifestation. Remember, you taught others to obey the Divine will, and your lives were devoted to that which you experienced as the Divine will. The new priests of my era – the astronauts, the divers of the deep sea, the physicists, the technological army of divine fools obeying what they feel and know is their destiny – will be as devoted to me as you thought you were in your time. Their souls will be as devoted to the New Ways as you and your followers were when you taught the doctrine of the Divine right of each individual to the spirit. So I say this Divine right has to be in the flesh as well as in the spirit. No deeper or more powerful descent of the spirit will be experienced by humans than in my kingdom."

"And no deeper or more powerful the Hell, once their worldly and technical pursuits are spent and they will have to face their spirit and the fact of the Christ within," adds Asterius, undaunted by the primordial power of this god. Stepping resolutely up to Aquarius, he continues, "Don't ever fool yourself with your heavenly fireworks. Your obstreperous spirit behaved like an old-fashioned Yahweh. We doubted your capacity and you were furious. Perhaps Isaiah I and after, Alfrenennon, might have been impressed, but we Christians of later vintage find such manifestations of power in poor taste and self-indulgent. Your thunder was not the thunder of change; it was a negative abomination of a god who ought to become better aware of his humanity. Show yourself with love or wisdom, then see how we react. Then we would be willing to suffer for your sake. Then we would become priests of your era, with all the added wisdom gathered from the last two thousand years of Christianity."

They stand facing each other, the older man and the young god, neither afraid. Thus challenged, wisdom rises in Aquarius. "Asterius," he says, and he tries to put his hand on Asterius' shoulder but fails, as the gesture is halfhearted. "Asterius, I stand corrected. There will be much pain and agony, and I know my entrance into this world will cause endless upheaval, for even the smallest flea will try to establish his right to bite, not realizing that every bite carries its own consequences. We will all become wiser, but the consequences will be terrifying. Every thought and idea will fight for its existence on this Earth."

As Aquarius speaks, the expression on his face becomes more and more sad, and he looks into the far distance as if to detect somewhere an answer which would mark the end of his road. What, what, oh Lord, can be the outcome of his earthly incarnation? For a moment he is like an old man looking to Christ for reassurance, but all he sees is Sophia, smiling her most mysterious smile. "Sophia," he cries out, "Mother of God, Wife to my Divine Essence, what will it be like?" And Sophia presents herself, as she often does when called upon with enough intensity and wish for truth. She sits down next to Aquarius, takes his right hand and while playing with his fingers says: "We don't know, Aquarius. Your reign, unless it is filled with love and wisdom, will be the most cruel experience of mankind, as the powers of good and evil will be equally divided. If you wish, I will marry you, and in our marriage a possible solution may be lived out in which humanity will be slightly more wise, slightly more tolerant, and a great deal more spiritual than now. However, this cannot be brought about unless close contact is sought with me."

September 12, 1966
Waverstead

They continue sitting, as if in council.

September 19, 1966
Waverstead

Reread a great deal

October 2, 1966
Waverstead

"Oh Mother Goddess, how can I? How can it be possible? I want to be married to younger ideas, to experiment, to experience what it is like to have direct contact with humanity. I will flee to you when I am in despair. I will go to you when I am curious and want to know what would be best. Wife of my Essence you are and always will be, but I don't want to live with my innermost being. I want to flirt with life and play my own game with humanity. I want to see what they do and what I want them to do, knowing that they are in my power as they were in Christ's power – either following, rebelling, or even indifferent to any ruling god. I want to be young and lighthearted.

"But humanity is not young and lighthearted any more, and our memories go deeper every day," a voice answers.

"Who says that?" asks Aquarius, startled. He looks around again and again and all he sees is a grey mist. Grey is everywhere. "Where are you all? What is happening? What is happening? Don't leave me alone." But, nothing happens. He is alone, and all is grey.

"Aquarius?"

"Yes. Who are you? Come out of the mist."

"Aquarius, I'm Erlo."

"Come out of the mist," says Aquarius.

"I am not in so dense a fog that you can't see if you want to."

"Who are you?"

"A human being who doesn't like to be experimented with."

"Why did they all leave?"

"They didn't. We are all here. You put yourself in a thick fog by talking like a foolish young man."

"Who cares?"

"I do, Aquarius. I served Christ and his period. Now I would love to have my new contact with you. Try to see me."

Aquarius looks, and encouraged by the deep sincerity and warmth he hears in the voice through the mist, he puts out his hand, even though he cannot see clearly. Then Aquarius and Erlo face each other.

"Have I seen you before?" Aquarius asks, hesitantly.

"No," Erlo answers. "Once you looked at me, but saw only the Christ in me."

"Where was that?"

"It was at the open place in the wall in the meadow. I was there when Christ's shadow tried to kill you. It was then Christ entered my body, and we shook hands – the three of us. But you saw only the Christ, not me."

Aquarius looks at Erlo, who is still vague in the mist. He extends his hand toward Erlo, who grasps it and neither lets go. As they stand there, the fog lifts and Aquarius sees Erlo clearly. He also sees a group of people behind him.

"Who are they, Erlo?"

"They are all me and my memories through the ages. Each of us, Aquarius, has his own memories. We have lived many lives. There is not a soul on earth, your earth, who does not have his ancestors, his roots. Tall or short, fat or thin, we are living souls, living flesh, and equal in the eye of God. You can be frivolous or young, inexperienced or wise – and I might be the same – but let us not play experimental games with each other of the kind that would spell disaster for both."

"What do you mean, mortal man? What games do you refer to?"

"That game of life which would deny my immortality; that game which would deny the voice of the spirit, or which would want to live in total ignorance of the flesh. As a god with a human countenance, you should know that neither spirit nor flesh can be denied; that both Heaven and Earth have to meet in us if we are ever to travel in harmony."

Slowly Aquarius lets go of his grip with his new friend and puts his hands behind his back. He looks at the group before him, wheels around on his heels and strolls away very slowly. "Give me some time, and don't go away, please," he says. Those words came hard; to be so polite and, at the same time, make such an appeal! After walking forward a few paces, the newly enthroned Aquarius turns around and with small, narrow eyes inquires inquisitively: "Do you mean to say that the New Age cannot be started with new, young spirits, and that the Earth is filled only with people connected to past ages who are embedded in ways of tradition and religion? Will my youth be spent with the ages past? What a trap! What devilish contrivance! Leave your past, leave it behind Erlo and follow me! Follow the new, the young, and the strong!"

"Young people will follow your new spirit blindly to their downfall. But those with experience and insight of the past will not follow so quickly, for they will never give up their hard-won treasures. Human nature, in all its complexity, will be influenced by you. But, Aquarius, the success and stability of your reign depend on the memory of our human race. Have they learned or forgotten the lessons of the past? Have the gods before you lived in vain? Should the followers of Buddha forget his teachings, or should they bring you their wisdom? Is the discipline taught by Confucius worthless, and the balance of the Tao non-existent? Are the Christians to forget the lessons of Christ, or the Jews to ignore the law of Moses? All of them have to unite under your banner. You know that! Didn't you tell me you are the Great Awakener, the Great Strengthener of all faith, and that through you the doors will open into the Hereafter? You said, 'For me, all worlds will melt into One. ... The Upper and Lower worlds will find their bridge so that All will be as One undivided world...'"

Aquarius looks quizzically at the group whose spokesman seems to have awakened his wiser side, then walks slowly and smilingly back and addresses the two Isaiahs.

"Does that idea sound familiar to you both?" Aquarius asks. "One spirit ruling this world; one Almighty effort and purpose. What will happen, do you think? Will humanity come closer to that vision? You had visions. I have mine, but it is really all up to Erlo, the mortal man, to discover to what extent they can be lived. He is on Earth. It is up to him, and the thousands and millions like him, to create with spirit and body the reality of a visionary moment. I feel heavy at heart now. I have watched humanity through all the aeons and there seems still such endless ignorance in me. May my reign give just that impetus to humanity to carry it over the next threshold, and may the host of devout spirits increase to aid our work. Turning to Erlo, Aquarius continues: "You, scribe for a host of people, will have to encourage and berate me perhaps, so that neither of us every forget our tasks as living spirits – I, as a god; you, as a human.

"Good night, gentleman. Take your rest." And smilingly, Aquarius adds, "I know I can ignore you now, but there seems to be plenty of spirit in what you supply to your spokesman. I better talk with Sophia and see if she is willing to receive an old god with new life coming up in him."

October 11, 1966
New York City

"Aquarius, are you knocking at my door? What do you want?"

"I need you. You gave your soul to Christ for nearly two thousand years; now I need it for the next two thousand years."

"I have already promised you my cooperation."

"That's not enough, my man, not enough. Your spirit is what I want."

"No. My spirit is my own. My life is my own and even God wants his independence."

"Yes, that is possible, but you don't allow me to penetrate your psyche. You don't allow enough of a mingling, a love affair, a marriage. The Mother Goddess and I cannot marry unless there is a marriage in you. I must have an experience of union with you, for only after your body is infused with my spirit will you know of my Being. My seed has to live in your spirit in a moment of Oneness with me, a moment of forgetting who and what you are and being One with me, Aquarius."

"Those big psychic experiences are always a terrible strain and something I fear."

"Without that union, my dear Erlo, nothing more can happen. Somewhere, at one moment in time, I have to be human. Otherwise, I will never know the individual, the human aspect of things. I will remain a god and never know what the human race is like. And don't think it is easy to find a human who is capable, let alone willing, of lending his body for the purpose of receiving a god. After all, you're not talking to a ghost. You are talking to the spirit which will rule for hundreds and hundreds of years. Just as Christ-Jesus needed a union with God the Father, so you need a union with me."

"Isn't it the other way around? You, Aquarius, have to square off with me."

"Someone has to be the first."

"I will be sick from it, and it will change my entire life."

"No, you will not be sick but it will change your life. Your life will be enriched and expanded. Furthermore, you have been prepared for it. The Mother Goddess tells me that she can do nothing with me unless you, Erlo, consent to a union. Then, she says, we can work on Earth to accomplish and incarnate the New Age. Jesus of Nazareth was the first for the Piscean Age, and his union with God the Father was on the cross. I am not of the order of the Piscean fish. The human sacrifice I ask is of a different nature. If the individual should die, I would fail in my purpose. My own Aquarian existence has to be established in life, but the qualitative and the quantitative, the unknown and the known, have to meet in me."

"Aquarius, what will be the task you demand?"

"A breakthrough into a world long forgotten, a very natural world against which a barrier was later erected. That earlier world enabled our conscious side to develop without too much interference from what you now call the world of the unconscious. My call for removal of that barrier does not mean a withdrawal into an archetypal world of mine. On the contrary, it means a coupling of human and spiritual forces which will create a new understanding of life. This new awareness will be apparent to you alone but soon understood by many who will be able to follow in your footsteps. They will follow the way many followed the spirit of the Christ, without either having to suffer the crucifixion or having to live as Jesus. Just following his example was enough. In this attempt lies the teaching which will bring about thc cvolution of spirit.

But who can teach who has not been taught? This sort of initiation is your nervousness today."

November 2, 1966
New York City

Almost a month has gone by since I wrote last in this book and much has happened. From the night of the 11th to the 12th of October, I loaned my body to Aquarius for about an hour. The recovery has been slow. Still, I have worked every day, which is a good thing. This momentous event was witnessed by my wife in this living world of ours; but how many were present from the other world we do not know. My wife prayed hard for Professor Jung's presence, and when it was all over we had the feeling that he might well have been there.

Thinking back to that night is still a difficult task. It is not the first time the spirit of an archetype has spoken through me. Also, on rare and emotion filled occasions, my wife has been with me when a part of my soul from the past relived a moment in time. Also, certain truths from bygone days have had to find a channel in me, so that I could become fully aware of the many aspects of my past lives. This process is always most painful and shocking to me; then, my rational side is rudely pushed away. It is most difficult for a stubborn Dutch-born man to give in to ideas of an irrational nature.

Thus it was on October 11th, when I sat on the sofa in our living room and my wife, in her large chair, sat next to the fireplace. Aquarius, as the reader knows from my writing, never took on the form of a man or a being I could visualize. It all happened, though, very differently from what I had expected.

In a fantasy, I see a round hole in the wall in our living room at the very place where a portrait of Paracelsus hangs, and I believe that through that round hole a fantasy-form will enter. A telephone call and a remark by my wife, however, interrupts the vision. For a moment only, I see an old man in a wheelchair trying to come in through the window. But he is pushed aside and the window closes. A faint form then sits in a chair in front of the painting. As I describe my imaginary thoughts to my wife and answer some of her questions, I notice a change in my voice and know immediately that I am hooked, for the change is a sign to me that I am not fully in control of myself anymore.

I straighten up, sit in the middle of the sofa and close my eyes; I don't want to be distracted anymore by anything present in the room. I know that only by deep concentration can I speak what I hear with my inner ear. In this way I sense subject and object; I sense a duality of existence, which I almost lost that night because I was so completely involved in what the spirit of Aquarius experienced in my body. Not for a moment during the following hours did I lose contact with my wife, or did I drop into any form of unconsciousness in which my ego was unable to record what the inner voice said.

November 3, 1966
New York City

Aquarius has much to experience and realize. Curiously, he feels all over my body; several times he taps at the base of my spine as well as up my back to the top of my head. Twice during the hour he touches my feet and toes, and at one time he explains how very similar we are, as if he expects me to be someone totally different or someone very strange. I have the feeling that my feet are the strangest part to him, and when I put my hands on my body I get the impression that the feeling contact is not the important one. It is as if he registers something in my body which he wants to find or recognize in himself.

Just before I sense that Aquarius is about to take over my body completely, a fantasy occurs in which my belly is ripped open from its base to just below the navel, and into this opening a black ball about four inches in diameter is inserted. I hear my unconscious say, "You will need this for stability. It will hold you and give you strength." Later on in the evening Aquarius mentions that he will put an eye in that black ball. As my hand feels my navel, he says with a smile, "There lives" or "here is the Mother Goddess."

I also remember Aquarius leaning forward, and then moving back, in a strange attempt to emphasize what he is saying. "There is no difference between Life and Death. It is all the same." He keeps on repeating these words, as if he is astonished about their truth. Now, as I write, I take his remarks very much as a statement of a god, one whose emphasis is totally centered in the psyche. It is a realization that occurs in him. Although I doubt my conscious side can fully accept this statement, it will be felt as a fact from the standpoint of my unconscious. My personality may have to do a lot of readjusting, perhaps, but not my Eternal Being.

November 19, 1966
New York City

I have refused to continue to write. There has been a violation of my personality, a ruthless, terrible undoing. If I never write down what Aquarius said to me in that hour, I don't care. It is not that my conscious side is revolting; nor that I feel an injustice has been done but, as a result of that visit, it is as if I am pushed deeper, much deeper into this world in a way I do not want.

This world has never been that enchanting to me, anyway. Perhaps the reason I don't dare to taste more of it is that I know the opposite side always has to be experienced. There seems to be a play in me which tries not to experience either pleasure or suffering too deeply, so that life is more bearable. I feel, too, that when I venture forward I create an unknown

Karma, and all that which was an unconscious drive has to be made conscious later – and that process can be very difficult. As long as I let life bring the events to me, I am not responsible. Would that make my Karma easier? I don't know, but I do know deep involvement in life is terribly, terribly hard for me and the powers coming through now are involving me deeper and deeper in this world. I resent, intensely, this push into life.

I came to this world first as Isaiah I, then as Isaiah II, the evangelical prophet, and that is where I am stuck and where my detachment began. In one of my dreams, I remember a female figure emerging from the top of a tree. She was tree-born, and I knew from this that she was (and is) the essence of my anima or spirit. She looked like a Persian princess, and was very detached from the world and from life. She had been living this way for a long time. You can see that detachment in me all through my Christian lives. Now, however, my anima is being pulled deeper and deeper into this world – and this is true only because of Aquarius. His power entering me is activating my unconscious to such an extent that I cannot stay detached any more. The Light of Darkness, with irresistible strength and allure, attracts my unconscious. This attraction must be the violation I feel. Although I will have to follow this pull, I fear its power very much.

No real aloofness from life is truly possible, I know, unless there has been a full experience and evaluation of it. Full involvement in life is the answer to release. There must be, somewhere within me, an immense importance attached to this earth-life, and I don't want to admit it. Perhaps the reason for such an attachment lies in sensing an enrichment of Being, which I can take with me to the other side. Could it be that this earth makes it possible for the soul to become more aware of its own Being? Could it be that here on this planet the laws of the universe can be better observed or dealt with – as if our body of flesh and blood is a miraculous alchemical laboratory where we can tangibly experience ourselves in a way more profound, more important, than in any other state of Being? It is here on earth that we bring an offering and take away a gift of Eternal Being. Is this the reason why we cling to life so hard in this most difficult and painful valley of tears? Is it here that we can realize and bring to fruition a consciousness so precious and important that it could truly enrich the Godhead, as well as ourselves? If so, it would be of the greatest importance to conquer space and reach for the moon, as well as to reach toward and travel into the dark spaces of the psyche or the human mind.

But I feel if I give in and enter this life with my fullest Being, while standing at the portals of the New Age, I will be forever linked to this earth. If I succumb, my earthly rounds – which have been held to a minimum – will multiply. I will be constantly involved in life on this planet and have to endure a round of incarnations from which I hold myself back out of fear and pain. There is no choice, I realize. I have to become entangled and embroiled, completely; the violence and intensity of doing so is my dread and fear. I will stop writing now and live with this thought for awhile to see what it entails.

November 22, 1966
New York City

My dreams have shown me that when I enter more deeply into this existence I will gather more strength in my instinctive being. While withdrawal from life brings about an anemic effect, the fullest participation in my work and daily life is animating. But oh, how I would love to float and stay detached from this world. Just to stay removed and aloof! I have seen people around me do it. (My father did.) As a rule their foreheads are wrinkled up high and their eyebrows stand in a wide circle around their eyes. While I have pitied them at times because of their suffering, I have also envied their remoteness.

Should I follow them? God forbid! Suffering without development is an abomination to me, and I fear that those dear people who float through life with their high eyebrows and wrinkled foreheads don't gain a thing. They lose their vitality and live in a world of partial accomplishment and constant anxiety. I know the truth of this last observation from my own detachment. Anxiety lives forever when we don't enter the foray; then we can neither win nor lose. I know enough now to realize that is why I have to enter the battle; in order to lose or to win. In either case, I gain awareness and consciousness and I stop floating. The constant change in life guarantees that, lose or win, the battle for greater understanding continues.

Now, most solemnly, and with a prayer for my daily bread, I will throw all of my life force into the battle, knowing that this commitment will entail many hardships but also realizing that my most inner Being will be tied in a deeper and firmer way to this planet Earth. So, I sit here at my desk on 71st Street deeply involved, hearing with one ear the New York City traffic and, with the other, listening to the life-song of the ages – a tragic melody drumming deeper and deeper into my soul that acceptance of life leads to the redemption and clarification of my Being. Tears, anxiety, but also a sense of triumph are present. My heart, therefore, is glad; my spirit rejoices and my flesh shall go in hope – and all these feelings coincide with a deep grumbling of earth, as if rocks tumble and fires glow in the nether world. One soul is now linked more deeply, more profoundly to the shivering, shaking elements of the underworld that is awaiting self-awareness and love for spirit.

So, spirit descends and earth rises to enter the battle of awareness. The cock is crowing; a New Dawn is upon us and the unutterable pain of birth rolls on further and further into the ages to come, but linked with the past and with the unutterable pain of sacrifice. Glory to God; the ego enslaved and embroiled by the Self. What pain! What glory! And I, Erlo, sign my contract with the powers that be to carry out what is mentioned above.

November 29, 1966
New York City

The pain of the ego's sacrifice prevents me from continuing to write about Aquarius. Although I know, by intuition, the truths I have recorded, I cannot emotionally digest them. The remoteness I feel in my anima is brought about by a sacrifice I made at another time and which, also, I am not able to digest.

A dream comes back to me. I am standing with some people in my immediate surroundings and there are some soldiers standing further away from me. I remember it is a place I have come to voluntarily. A glass of water, crystal clear, is in my right hand and beyond me a little, to my right, is a long, shallow pit with bars over it and a glowing fire underneath. It is where I am to be sacrificed. The soldiers are not anxious to go through with the sacrifice, but all of us know it has to happen. I drink the pure water and give this toast: "To Israel!"

This sacrifice, symbolized by the toast of clear water as a pure conscious act, was the essence of my writing – as Isaiah II – pertaining to the sacrifice of the one for the many. In my soul, there is still a deep, dark gash. I was able, then, to live out the extremes of both the Dark and the Light side of Being because my entire poetic soul was so deeply involved in that life. It was not until I lost my beautiful, strong, and firm body of Jewish-Egyptian origin that I realized the ghastly wrench which had taken place. The pain of the body is forgotten. Forgotten, or better, forgiven, is my post-mortem beheading and having my head shown to the high priests as the last male descendent of the Sait Pharaohs. The Persians could rule; there was no fear of an Egyptian resurrection or revolt. The unutterable pain was in my spirit; my soul cried out. This incarnation, this expression of the flesh which had written with such compassion, "Comfort ye, Comfort ye" – where was its comfort? In a most sadistic way, the darkness of God's earth demanded a kill.

But the magic of Isaiah II, the unknown prophet, was already among the people. Before the sacrifice took place, he had been spurred to his most beautiful writings. He had still believed in the goodness and the strength of the Lord, in his immense greatness, despite the fact that all existing power had fallen now into the hands of conquerors, petty priests and vainglorious armies. Through his writings, though, the nation was set at rest. The soul of Israel had become the soul of its despised servant, and the "Servant Songs," which he wrote, had become the country's deepest expression.

But would my soul ever have a more beloved son, a more beautiful instrument? Afterwards, as Antiochus the Great, I raged and killed – as if slaying could satisfy me. I learned. Yes, I learned about life through all that slaughter, but I never, never overcame my horror of earth-living. As Asterius, my homilies were very much in vogue for some five or six hundred years. As Walter and Wilfred, I lived powerfully, helping to bring about order and law. But, as Walter, I was often vindictive and had to learn my lesson painfully. Then, as François Fénelon, I wrote in a very popular way. And now, Aquarius calls and knocks at my door reviving the pain of Isaiah II, the evangelical prophet, and a true Piscean. Never again will I express myself like him or write with such conviction; that was another time. Neither shall I ever again be like Isaiah I; that was the first descent, full of archaic life and insight. Now I write as Erlo, a composite of all these figures, who is scarred and wounded but aware that when I integrate the sacrifices I have suffered and realize that they were necessary expressions in their time, I will cure myself by going ahead with all the knowledge I have gathered. Slowly, I will heal my wounds with what Aquarius will bring to the surface in me.

The great message Aquarius revealed to me on the night he took possession of my body was this: without the Christ spirit, all is lost. The dark and black side of life can no longer be repressed – but neither will the light and white side – and in the battle between them our only guide will be the existence of the Christ symbol within us. The black side is not, by itself, evil and dangerous, for it contains as its center, Lucifer, the Light Bearer. Because he is the Left hand of God, he does not obstruct consciousness but rather brings consciousness to our shadow world. The Christ, as the symbol of the Right hand of God, has now matured to the place where he will not deny, as Jesus had to do, the dark Lucifer. If we lived eternally on this earth in our bodies, there might be different laws; as our mortality is one of the great prices we pay for our wisdom, immortality exists only where there is consciousness.

I, Erlo, suffered the Light of Lucifer in the death of Isaiah II. I survived, but terribly, terribly crippled. However, when I have the strength to suffer that Light, I know I can bring back into eternal consciousness a Light which shines brighter than any star ever did. It will be a Star of Bethlehem; may God give me the strength for it. Unknown to me, right now, this prayer is being answered as I write my gospel.

December 17, 1966
New York City

For some weeks, I have been recuperating from the effects of the experiences I have written about. What comes up in my mind, now, is the moment when I open my eyes the night Aquarius houses himself in my body.

Prior to that instant, I keep my eyes closed for a considerable time in order to listen and to experience what is lived by my visitor as far as I can register it, both in thought and in deed. Then comes the moment to open my eyes; it is a moment of birth. I have the feeling that something irrevocable is going to happen; a farewell and an encounter at the same time; a union of opposites, after which neither spirit nor matter will be the same; a marriage, birth, and death in one. It is the moment of the inevitable incarnation. Human emotions are at a peak – expectations are high, but there are no tears. In a second it is done and I see our living room again. All is the same there, but within me all is different. The inner change has happened to me, and both my mortal and immortal sides are affected.

I remember fixing my eyes at the top of the curtains and the ceiling, not daring to blink; those eyes have to stay open for two thousand years. There is a repetition, I believe, of Aquarius' prophecy that I wrote in Holland, and then came the great revelation that the Christ principle is to act as the guiding light in the New Age.

But it was through the suffering of Alfrenennon's death that I digested Lucifer's Light and a deeper level was reached. It was not until the day after Thanksgiving, on Friday, November 25th, that I dreamt of the song of the beauty and fragrance of Israel. The song in the dream is about the intense sweetness and beauty of some flowers discovered by a traveler or explorer. These flowers are tall and slender, but dried up. Lord help me, I write when I awake in the middle of the night, for the song is so moving. All of the song is in French, so I think François is the messenger and the last one to hear it before it reaches me.

The devil is not far away, however, for that afternoon after a nap in our country home, I hear the words clearly in my ears: "*Je veux la gloire, la reconnaissance.*" These words, the very opposite of what Isaiah II wanted during his life on earth, signify that there is a clamoring now for the other side of the coin. This other side, indeed, comes up the steps of the Ladder of Unlived Life from ages past and has to be recognized and digested. It belongs very much to Aquarius, for on the night of his coming he could not get over the fact of how human he was, how much like us he was in his own feeling. Also, my dreams and experiences show how closely connected we are with that which we think is dead and gone, but is not.

"There is no difference between Life and Death; it is all the same," Aquarius says. So, in part of our Being we have to and can relive all in our past that could not be experienced in order to bring it to the light of consciousness. And what is the light of consciousness but the fusing of the Light of Day and the Light of Night, the fusing of the Light of the Christ and the Light of Lucifer, or the spirit of the Heavens as seen by us and our Earth existence as experienced by us. I remember Aquarius' curious statement, "You see, I was the Christ and not the Christ; I was the development of Christ and of God also." And then came his remark of the crucial importance of following the Christ principle. That revelation was the moment of identification and recognition that All is One, All is the Lord's creation. How very Isaian! How timeless!

Sunday, January 8, 1967
New York City

"Oh Erlo, dear Erlo, where have you been hiding? The nights are pitch-black and the days have lost their shine. All through the Christmas holidays and the New Year there was darkness in my heart, for you dance and dine far away from my Light. Chandeliers and candlesticks serve as your light, a light of sad glory. While I know there was warmth and love for wife and friends, I am jealous for the Lord, jealous of time spent away from his new glory, the New Age to come."

"Isaiah," I shout, "where are you?" But Isaiah is asleep, hiding away, withdrawing, for his prophetic sense – now so matured during the millenniums – sees the debacle of the solstice.

"Neither are you, mortal scribe, willing to listen to my message," Aquarius continues. "My descent is not a temporary event to be followed by a physical death and a spiritual resurrection. I didn't come down to withdraw from the world. I am here to reign as king, to postulate, to be, to teach and be taught. Through you, Erlo, I married this world, and will not be divorced or separated from it out of your fear of me. I need your roots – your Isaiahs, your prophets – again and again. I long for this ancient Isaian alignment to spiritual truth which you have, without the concoctions of a civilized mind; this basic contact with my divine Being is what I need. Let theologians, psychologists, and philosophers think whatever they want about me, but to you, Erlo, I address myself to the glory of a vision of divine portent.

"It is not necessary, my dear scribe, for you to be correct, to be historically correct. It is divinity, divinity of life which is the only worthwhile and deeply touching aspect of existence, and most loved by me, your god, your Christ, your Aquarius. The Isaiahs were not copied, printed, and reprinted because they made worldly prophecies which never came about. Their prophecies were not so important in comparison to the ideas they perceived concerning the greatness and goodness of God. Although your god loves his incarnation, his physical manifestation of a small part of his Being, he needs to mirror his Essence in the Diamond surrounded and made numinous by the darkness of the Abyss. And why would his Essence not include the Abyss? It does. For in the Abyss he can hear about humanity's despair of living, more precious to him than his Essence, or perhaps that is his Essence; your suffering maybe is his Jewel."

"Oh, that it may be so."

"It is so, my scribe and teacher of human misery. In all of the Christmas glitter you were lost to me, but what a lovely and good time it was for you! As I stood by looking on at your celebrations, I learned and realized how the rejoicings of the divine can become lost in the delights of the body. Yours is a true marriage, I know. The jubilation is not wrong; it is right. The families, friends, and relations were all celebrating, in carnal ways, the ways of the spirit. Memories are made and relived, earthly ties are strengthened and a peace is brought about in which the world takes its place and claims its own for the sake of the spirit. What other way is there for those who truly live in this world? But I, your god, your spirit, can only learn about my descent into the carnal through a suffering which brings me consciousness. So your Christmas celebration was deep darkness for me, and the food, the wine, the laughter all brought a pain in the loins to me – an emerging god. I know I am a god; I am spirit. I know you, Erlo, are both spirit and human, and therefore more privileged. With your duality my consciousness can grow. You can become the real messenger, the direct link to the Godhead, my Father, and our Creator.

"Scribe, I pray now to you, mortal man with an immortal spirit. In facing the future together with me, dare to see. Use the roots that are yours. Build on the immortal side of your Being, and give me your attention and energy in a measure commensurate with your true Self. The frailty of the human race is heavily dependent upon its vision of spiritual greatness. All outer distinction is the banality of little men. Those who have the capacity to endure the destruction of their ego, those alone are capable of visualizing a greater world. You, as Isaiah, named them many centuries ago – the men who God 'calls upon.' Many more are called upon than ever before, and many more will become the 'chosen ones.' They are the ones whose vision will illuminate the earth. So, I pray, stay close to me; speak with me so that I may speak with you, and as you teach me I will reveal my vision to you and, if consciousness permits, my reality. But of the two, vision is greater, for through vision reality is pruned and lived with differently and bears greater fruit.

"Oh, come to me, my beloved son and teacher. Walk with me through the centuries past and I will show you a vision of the centuries to come. Walk with me so that the rhythm of our steps together will become the bells of destiny, sounding loud enough to awaken those who are asleep and ignorant of their fate and the beauty of their Selves. Let our steps make the earth tremble and quake in anticipation of the years to come in which endless opportunities may illuminate the minds of men. Keep step with me, my scribe, lest we disturb the dead of the accomplished deed, who sleep in God's bosom awaiting resurrection. Let our steps harmonize all that is misunderstood and so bring harmony to a world bloodily laden with unconscious behavior and short-sighted sin. Let our steps be as gentle as the wind penetrating the woods and bending the grass to its will. Then, perhaps, our painful hours together will bear fruit in the age to come. So, write on my scribe. Live with me, and I with you. Amen."

January 15, 1967
New York City

What can it be? What can it be that makes me so despondent, so terribly shaken? Have I not done any analysis? Have I not wept my eyes out about my parents, my family and the hurts of my life? What can smart so dreadfully still, as if I were killed and had to go on living. After a night of deep contact with my soul, my father was shown to be a hard, spiritless Jew. Now, it is as if the tears shed over that dream have to melt the hard core of a bitter, bitter part of me that was so forsaken, so horribly crippled, that no spirit could penetrate. What law is at work? What crime has been committed? My sarcasm goes deep, hating and blaspheming God for his utter stupidity in creating this human world.

Endless, endless is the pain I feel. But this pain is just me, just who I am – Erlo! The pain is just me. I was crucified unknowingly and now, years later, I am becoming aware that I have been fucked, screwed – but by what? By whom? It is as if in the middle of the night came the rapist, who raped and raped and didn't leave a trace behind, only a mutilated body. I am that victim. Somewhere I have been so wronged, so violated that I don't want life to come through any more. But it is just my wish – Erlo's wish. And what does that mean in the scheme of things? Nothing! Nothing!

May 27, 1967
Zürich

Mighty are those who humble themselves before the Lord, whose son, Aquarius, is to rule for the next two thousand years. Lay down your crop of bourgeois clothing, and sooner gird yourself with the wickedness of Sodom and Gomorrah. Nothing can happen to you by way of the properness of morality, for the power of the Lord is kept in bondage by the pettiness of proper living. Away with normalcy, lest you poison your soul with decency and forget the mercurial spirit which transcends your moral, balanced, everyday living. Vicious is the moral towards the spirit; the Light of Darkness, Lucifer, is held in bondage, which is as bad as the absence of Christ.

Spirit has to live and you, Erlo, filthy swine, try to smother it with decency and honor and integrity. Now, in time, those outmoded, worn out principles have to be left behind, for the Aquarian cannot occupy himself with good alone. Without darkness there is no life. Your highly cultured sophistication is the fibre which has to be used so differently. It has been tempered through the ages, but now is requested to bear fruit in the darkness as well as in the sunlight of life. Your black brother, Tom, is your key. So are your crusaders and Eusebius, the evil one, who in their thoughtless ignorance all used, or better misused, the power of darkness to further their goddamn egos. But now use that evil for the purpose of life itself. Be aware of people and watch out for their shadow. Use power for your spirit, so it can live and express itself. Light and Darkness forever more.

If you are offended, son of Pisces, the displeasure you feel is your own shortcoming, for the shadows of Darkness have to be cleansed as well as the shadows of Light, which were cleansed so well earlier in your writings. The descent into Hell at this time of history is more actual and of greater importance than even Dante wrote about. There's nothing poetic about that journey. Tom will lead you down as his greed and weakness for power, which is nothing but lack of spirit, was not recognized by him at all. He withdrew in darkness and didn't come to the light which shines in it.

You must enter into the Pit, Erlo. You must let your balls burn with the Holy Fire, for the power of evil is everywhere and you don't see it at all. How can you lead people, as you have to, without experiencing the immense importance of blackness which supports all earth-living? You, of the spirit, will fail unless you comprehend dense psyche; that is to say, flesh and blood. On that level, low quality words are spoken but they are not foul. They are most basic; they are plant-like and bestial, but also as divine as the words of Christ.

Know that the flesh and the spirit can be liberated. The streets of Jerusalem ran with blood of the Saracens, and you, Erlo, were the murderer. You misused the Black, as you misused the Light. You were so far in the heavens that you thought, most erroneously, you could overrule the flesh. So, you murdered the flesh; you took bodies and mutilated the sacred flesh. But how will you – how will I, the great Isaiah – know anything of earth unless the cries of the souls' slaughter is heard and the blood of others on my hands is smelled. The heavens were rent with the cries of the slain bodies and Christ himself, with a sardonic smile on his face said: "How I erred. My blood on the Cross was not enough. Now, my misunderstood spirit fights with the sword and, after the first millennium, teaches me that the Black Fish is present, too. My Dark Brother is teaching my lesson, my life, and makes me realize he is part of my soul, also. And Peter, himself, is slaying the innocent and returns to the Darkness of life to learn."

How cruel! How cruel is life, is God, am I, Erlo! Grant me consciousness, oh Lord, so that the blood unleashed has not been painting the Holy Town red for vanity alone. Give meaning to this bloodshed. No. I will have to extract it myself, for unless I do, God will not. He is numb in his wisdom, unless I become more aware. He will not be able to comprehend. That is why he sent me here, for I experience his life as lived on earth. That is why I am, and that is why I am here now and will be here, always.

Suddenly, from within, I hear Jesus crying out, "Peter! Peter! You are my rock and evil is with it and part of it. Still, you penetrated the rock with my Light. I, Jesus, could not do so. I was all Light. I was the Christ. You, Peter were the entrance to the rock and carried my life forward. How dark the world had to become before we met the Light of Darkness as counterweight and balance of God's Being."

June 26, 1967
Zürich

The Unlived Life

Deeper than the Pit of Hell; deeper than life itself is the pain which rises from me to bring back human life to this earth. Never, never did I think such pain could be endured. The trees cannot contain it, Erlo; the thunder cannot relieve the burden of your soul. But while you walk the woods of the Zürich Dolder, the angels pray you can endure again the tearing of the flesh, the denial of the doomed, the rejection of the Unlived. No music descends from the heavens, only mute cries emanate from beneath the earth to reveal to you the agonies of the world's souls living in denial. The beautiful tone and mood of the clocks of Zürich do not reach the Damned Divine of life below – the Saints of Blackness, the Angels of Doom, the destructive souls of eternal unknowing.

Oh Lord, Lord! When, oh when, will your divine Aquarius come to give us strength and courage to carry this load? What agonies will have to be experienced in order for us to live out the miseries of these Dungeons of Hell? Will all this blackness have to incarnate? Will all this doom have to be made flesh and tortured into consciousness? Who? Who will have the strength to endure it and believe in God's tolerance? Where will be his grace and bounty? Who will dare to abide the day of his coming? When all is suffered, where will we be? When your Pit of Unlived Life is opened, will there be an end? Will we ever know that we are born to your Glory? Where, oh Lord, is the beauty of your creation, when so dark and stark a life is experienced? Will there be no end to our tears? Answer! Answer! Don't just stand there in amazement of such profound pain, unaware that man can suffer so deeply your divine creation of doom and not living.

I will not die. I will not fail myself on account of such pain. My ship cannot be wrecked for now, in this moment of absolute doom and darkness, a memory comes to me of when I entered your body, oh Lord, a memory of when the powers of life itself shook my body and your might well-nigh slew it. I remember when the love of every moment and every movement was revealed, and the two sides of your Being took hold of me to be reborn in the suffering of my shaken soul. Then it was that my temple of flesh and blood nearly crumbled and I was reduced to a tottering man on the edge of the abyss of another death. But this death of the Unlived, which I have endured for centuries and aeons and which now is budding into daily life, this yoke I know I must, and can, carry.

I will continue to live, oh Lord, not for your glory but for my own – and so, perhaps, too for yours. Through this suffering I will be reborn to the tasks of today. Through this Pit of Hell I will find my stable footing, and again you can call me the "rock," the rock of Peter. I will be then, again, like all of us who, Christ-born first, will have to be led to the birth of the stone. So be it; this round of life through the ages will be Christ, Rock – Christ, Rock. We will carry both aspects in us, according to our own strength and weakness; one will be as vital to our Being as the other. They will be inseparable fighting their way into consciousness.

Aquarius, do you listen? Embrace the Christ. Take him into your home so you may learn that the pain of the ages past is the flower of the present. Future! Oh future, where art thou? Elusive place of our vision, of our hope and relief, descend into the present and mix your illusion with the reality of the

Now. Then you might bring us peace and strength, and belong to the structure of the Now, which always is; the unfailing Now – Timeless – World without end and All-Embracing. The Lord be praised.

Through all this outpouring, Professor Jung sits next to me in the other chair. This crisis is hard, and so I will go slowly about my life, deeply thankful to him for his help, kind smiles and touching of hands.

July 9, 1967
Bad Ragaz

For over a year, I have been writing off and on in my notebooks, and today I sit at my window in the hotel Schloss Ragaz, again ready to put pen to paper. I can see the mountains with their patches of snow, the clouds moving in and out and around the barren peaks, the golf course below with its tiny figures moving, and further, I can see the village of Mainenfeld strewn over the hillside in little clusters of separate farmhouses. I can hear the far-off noise of passing automobiles – and there is always a bird singing, it seems. So, here I am, taking up my writing again. My dreams have plainly shown that it is high time to begin again as my riches, otherwise, will be misused in the banalities of life. My fruitfulness will be without spirit – neither good nor evil.

I seem to be unwilling to start writing, most likely on account of sadness, although Ann and I are in this beautiful place where we take the baths and the outside world has been offering us such a pleasant entourage. The inner picture has been difficult however, because my weak legs, psychically speaking, have been taught to stand more on their own feet. I have had friends who could help me many, many times with their knowledge, or kindness, or love. Now I have to know that in every person there is an area where nobody, nobody can help anymore. In that place a test of strength occurs which we seem to pull towards us, as if we need that challenge to find out if we can stand alone. It makes me think of the Bible story of Jacob wrestling with the angel; a test of strength in which the Lord wants to know, is this man I have created really capable of self-support? The angel sent to me was about as rough with me as he was with Jacob. I only hope that I won't limp after this fight.

My story really started this spring. For a long time I could not write as dreams, events, and a very busy professional life kept me on the go. Rereading my notebooks of January and February, I saw in what terrible straits I was being led. My contact with Aquarius had deepened my personal life and I can see, upon looking back, in what terrible dark hole I was put. I know now it was the Pit of Unlived Life under the altar of Asterius of Amasia. I am sure that is true because on a most beautiful, charming evening a piece of magic was performed on me.

During the celebration of my wife's birthday, a delightful parody of my professional life was enacted by clients of mine. The take-off was altogether enchanting to me, a charming piece of nonsense which put my personality under the scrutiny of Shakespeare, Dante, and Aeschylus at the same time. It must have been something like that because the next day, while getting up from sleep, I had a vivid fantasy of a round block of ice exploding in a thousand pieces, revealing a round hole in the ground. I knew that explosion and its revelation was the result of the magic play. Nothing of my persona was left intact that night, and I had laughed from deep, deep within about the frivolities of my life acted out in front of me with great mirth and love. The Hole to the Underworld was opened; my personal unconscious could receive now in form what I had suffered only vaguely the preceding months. The formless could now take shape and the agonizing suffering could be made into a personal experience. Of this tomorrow. But I am glad I am writing again to you, my readers of the future.

July 15, 1967
Bad Ragaz

Yesterday, a year ago, I began to write this book, and just yesterday Ann and I drove into the Alps to Arosa, a beautiful name for a commercial village in a beautiful setting. Today, I have to start writing about the dark, black side of life. It will be like writing about the endlessness of beauty, of which we know so little, except that we know still less about the endlessness of the dark.

For centuries we have read about the greatness of the Lord and have associated it with all that was uplifting, powerful, glorious, and sublime. The saints and savages alike have spoken about the wonders of creation and always seemed to couple these wonders with the surpassing spirit of Being. But this greatness of beauty was realized away from this earth. Eternal beauty and truth were relegated to the Light of the Godhead, and God's great Shadow was endowed with all that was mean and petty and vile.

And in that mean little place, in that vile position, I put myself many, many times – all through the ages of the past. Never did it occur to me how very one-sided this position was. So, part of me was relegated to the unknown darkness. My little evils, my ego wishes, even my personality was looked at askance, for all did not belong to the glorious, uplifting spirit of Christianity. That such a point of view, in itself, is evil was something I didn't know. But I learned through bitter, bitter emotional hardships and experiences. I learned. I learned and became aware of myself and my own Being, aware of the fact that without darkness there is no light, that without evil there is no good.

Oh Lord, forgive me when I write in my utter ignorance: why? Why did you create this horrible, painful human duality? Why couldn't we stay with you in your Oneness? Couldn't you experience yourself in your own Being without creating us, representatives of your Being on earth? What split you? Why am I, created in your image, living in duality? Why does the sun set, and night is then a blackness relieved only by a reflected, dead celestial body?

"Oh son, oh son, don't ask for truth when you are not prepared. But if you think your pain can be relieved by my knowledge, I will tell you. In bringing my spirit to earth in your being, I had to experience my own creation on a deeper – or was it a lower level? The cosmic God, which I am, has all in him; all creation is mine. So, as I had not known about the powers of my own depth, I prayed for consciousness of my own awareness. Thus, Sophia was born, the all-knowing wise aspect of myself, and there occurred the split, the duality, created out of love for knowing.

"In that duality you live now. It is so inherent in nature, in my Being, that I am always deeply perturbed about all those who forget about the Darkness or the Light, who forget about the ever-changing Being that I am. I am the only everlasting is, which IS always. All religions, all philosophies without this duality are one-sided, limping efforts to come to my presence. Such teachings may possess a glimpse of my Light, but little can that Light illuminate existence. When your icecap was shattered into vapor, the gate to your own blackness was opened. What was revealed was not just the blackness of this life, on which you have worked already so much, but also the Blackness of all the lives of the past connected with the shadow of your soul. This revelation will open your eyes to what a Shadow truly is, and that is what you didn't know and had to know if the meaning of Darkness and its divine message is ever to make any true impression on you."

July 16, 1967
Bad Ragaz

"In your first descent to this earth Erlo, as Isaiah, about 700 B.C., you came as a shining white light declaring the Glory of God and His Almighty Power," an inner voice announces. "As you had witnessed his greatness in your first vision, you could now inspire greatness and goodness all around you. Not that the people at the time thought too much about your visions and your prophesies. Most of them didn't listen. They simply could not, for just as you identified with the Glory of God and his shining goodness and were in the grip of his shadow, so were the others. But you saw this. You soon became aware that only a remnant can hold onto the vision of the Glory of the spirit while the rest of the population would be concerned mainly, if not only, with the value of their belongings and the power they bring. Seven hundred years had to go by before your Emmanuel could manifest himself in the person of the Christ Jesus, the maiden's Son, who would bring his Light to the people, albeit very, very slowly."

Yes, I hear all this. I, as Isaiah, was only a voice in the wilderness. I know. I have heard. The bells of the towers and the call to prayer of the minarets have sounded in vain, were it not for the remnant of souls who come back, time after time, to restate what the times need to save humanity from their worldly possessions in which they like to smother their divine spirit. Oh Lord, I know. And it cannot be different. Of late, I have learned that more than ever. My thoughts flew out wide over the masses; my visions, inspired by my fervor to proclaim the Glory of God on earth, have been heard and repeated many times. But they were only acted upon when the shambles of daily life forced the people to look upward. And when they did, floating through the skies were my thoughts, tainted red with the glow of burnt farms and possessions. Among the ruins of the castles, the people began to think of the possibility of transforming the sword into the plow. But no sooner were the riches of the plow everywhere, then there appeared the sword of greed and wickedness, and my vision was undone again. My only hope was, as always, an is now – my only hope lies in the remnant. The Wailing Wall would tumble if I would lean my despair against it.

There is, however, a law greater than I can ever express which will surpass all of my former visions of God and his greatness. That law was hidden from me and was not comprehensible earlier. But it was in your voice Lord, when you said, "Make them deaf, lest they hear. Make them blind, lest they see." That moment, when the people are not hearing, when the people are not seeing anything from without – that moment is a terrible crisis, for then will they, or can they, register their own inner voices and see their own inner Being. So blind them, oh Lord. Deafen them with their own iniquities. Then, let them go. Don't protect. Don't bless. Create a Nothingness of Being. Then, oh Lord, we humans face ourselves and we fall or we go on. We fall when we fail to detect our Being. We go on when, from within, rises that very core which we call now our Living Essence. When that happens, then perhaps there will be more than a remnant of souls surviving; there will be an army to the Glory of Being.

I know, I know what this means for haven't I been killed time after time to be resurrected? I descended in ignorance of the Glory which is earth. I was all spirit and there was little need in me for the "goodies" of this earth. I spoke with great conviction and fervor, and what I said was true, or became so later on. But how inexperienced I was then in comparison to how much I know now. I knew little about the Shadows of Death, the people who walk in Darkness. I had to suffer many lives in order to become more acquainted with pain and sorrow.

All of your creation, Lord, as I realize now, contains the very tools to self-awakening and understanding. No wonder that the end of my life came with the cruel death of having been sawed in two. I was only aware of the glorious possibilities of an exalted soul, and from the depth of darkness arose the duality necessary for comprehension. Utter bewilderment and unbearable suffering of flesh came upon me when I experienced the other reality which was there also, the reality called forth by ignorance of my own Shadow – God's shadow. For as I proclaimed the Light of the Heavens, the Darkness of Earth opened itself.

So, into the deepest Darkness I descended to meet the smiling face of a man, and – oh no, it was not true! It could not be! Once before I had looked upon the face of the Lord sitting on his heavenly throne and now, here, I recognized, to my unspeakable horror, his face again, smiling and benevolent looking, inviting me to his heart with outstretched arms. That was the moment, because of unbearable pain, I fainted in His arms and peace came to me.

July 18, 1967
Bad Ragaz

Tomorrow we leave Ragaz, then return for two days to Zürich, and then go on to Holland. The Swiss chapter is closing; a painful episode of learning comes to an end, and the future looks harder to me. Sadness fills my heart, which feels heavy with burdens and tasks. I am grateful for the beautiful setting, but I feel betrayed by a friend, and for a moment, my marriage rocks like an earthquake. Vacation, I have not had. My duty has been performed, and I have to watch that my sadness does not turn into bitterness. I sign off, heavy of heart, but will try to look pleasantly towards the future. My marriage, I feel, is the only beauty left. This traveler is weary.

August 4, 1967
On the Ocean

The Call to Greatness or True Being

Yesterday, after writing in my dream book, I came to understand that I had brought a painful message to one of my dearest friends and a beautiful soul. I became aware of the fact that my own consciousness is the teacher, that what I have lived myself and digested brought an unknown vista to my friend. So, from my position as pupil, I became teacher as well. This was a great revelation to me and made me realize more about my position in this world.

From dreams, I know that I will be called upon. The black man of the ocean had his dream. The stage is being prepared, and I tremble at the idea of coming forth and playing my role, lest it has to do with the Negro in the street. For I fear that black man of the sea; I know his fire is from within and is burning now on the outside. He wants to destroy his world; that desire is not wrong. His blackness has him by the throat and it is a fearful, heinous monster now. If he ever has the power to make it positive and of this world, then he will have a way of living.

Lord, have mercy on me, for I am most reluctant to face the blackness: "But your dreams are full of such portent – your black man of the sea; your grey man of the unlived; your black room which you had to descend from to meet the people of darkness without eyeballs; your dark man, your fear as he breaks into your homes in your dreams. There is a call, a great call – an awareness in you will attract it," responds a voice from within.

I fear. I fear. "You have to answer the call and then the reply will be put in front of you. You cannot settle your life on a small basis. It has to be decided on a greater scale and how that will come about will be shown in time. Only you must be prepared so that you can recognize the moment when the spark burns."

August 5, 1967
On Neptune's Pond

"Aeons and aeons have passed since I expressed myself freely and lustily on this globe of yours – aeons of silence and deep darkness in which, in ever increasing numbers, the unlived gathered in the cellars of the human mind. One, only one, is the doorkeeper to these gates of Hell and damnation and destruction. One, only one, holds the keys in both hands. Cross those keys and knoweth not what thou unlocketh. Similarly, cross the ways of life and live in the middle design created by the keys of Heaven and Hell. In the mandala formed by those keys are the four triangles and the fifth point.

"Keeper of the keys, awake to your destiny! Awaken to the fullest glory of the task ahead! Vision, or no vision – gold, or no gold, your personal task has to be accomplished. The wishes of the ages are the demands of the day. Slowly, slowly gather yourself. Remember the past and what was projected upon you; this projection still holds true to the life of the psyche. We, the unknown, the unlived salute you and beg for your Light and leadership. Your healing hand and mind will be our glory. From the Dark with us will arise a new spirit of earth realities, unknown to mankind and to the glory of your personality. I, Isaiah, am called again. I, Aquarius, will direct and produce. You, Erlo, sign your contract and so finish this book."

Erlo van Waveren promises his share, for better or for worse. *Deo Volente*.

November 25, 1967
Waverstead

Last Wednesday, it broke through. Ann and I were seated in the living room of our New York City townhouse, and I knew I could not hold back. The night before I had been weeping terribly, and now this horrible pain was in me again. My entire personal unconscious was caught in two ways: first, in a confrontation with the Buddha and second, in the recognition and acceptance of my total Being in a new role. Professor Jung was there in no mean way. I called on him, as I was badly in need of a supporting presence. I knew that in me there was not only Christ-Erlo, but also Buddha-Erlo; a living Buddha as well as a living Christ. That awareness was terrifically important because the universality of Aquarius was brought out; it was as if the message carried by me was not just for the West but for the East also.

After that recognition, I had a conversation with an aspect of Professor Jung which at first I did not understand. But a fantasy helped me greatly. In order to convince me that his life work was a preparation for my life work, Professor Jung knelt in front of me and showed deep reverence for the spirit which has to manifest in me. Later on, Professor Jung appeared as if he were dual. Although he sat in the chair he often sits in, which is under the painting of Paracelsus in our living room, a smaller Professor Jung also appeared who had the face of a sun, manes of a lion. He was kneeling in front of me saying: "My life was lived for you who has to carry the manifestation." Then the spirit took me and in a loud voice I shouted: "I am that living example," and repeated it several times. It was almost as if Professor Jung had said it through me, but I knew it was a complete fusion of all of me which burst forth, as if the entire power of Professor Jung was behind me. By my shouting, "I am that living example," I mean the living example of an Aquarian.

One of the aspects that arose from this fantasy was Aquarius came about through a marriage in man (an inner marriage), as if that condition was of great importance. Also, the fantasy revealed I have to live a life of direct action and seem to have a personality just fit to carry that out. Professor Jung said that for nine years there would be further preparation, but I know so well during this time that I will have to live with the fact of being a living example of a divine, new, most human god starting his reign. Through me will come clarification and comprehension for the ages to come, which will be different from the awareness born of Professor Jung. The differences are yet unknown to me but they will be revealed, of that I am sure and, according to my dreams, they will come through Professor Jung himself.

Another dual aspect of Professor Jung came up when in fantasy he appeared large and dark, told me to move over an sat on my right on the sofa. He said he could and would teach me more about the Dark side of life. I felt very good and was grateful for this new found strength, for he knew more than I about the Shadow and the Black side of life.

The entire evening was full of tears and deep psychic drama and was hard to live through. Now I know that I am not allowed to forget. I have always loved to tuck away the fact of being a living example of the New Age. My voice has deepened the last few days and somewhere I'm truly turning into myself. Ann told me this afternoon Professor Jung had said to her that evening that I was well protected. I remember, now, at times during the introversion I felt an aura around me of space and of angelic forces.

December 21, 1967
New York City

On this darkest of days, I have to write about my shortcomings. More and more am I being forced to live a life commensurate with my inner state of affairs, and less and less am I allowed to be the person I want to be. I don't want to be as I am, and that I know is very dangerous. But what I am told I am and really sense to be true is so hard for me to realize that I automatically push it aside after I finish writing. My mind has to be on the reality of what the Self wants, and I should not turn away from that. Constantly, constantly I try to belong to this world on my terms; I try to conform to my ego wishes. I am allowed, at times, still to do so, but stronger forces are at work. Unless I give in to that Real Plan, that true attempt of my soul to establish itself as a rounded out figure who is aware of his psychic roots, who is using all of his personality – unless I do that, my life will be lost and void. This is mighty serious, for what I have invested in this life is already considerable and

I would be loath to let go of such a vigorous attempt to stay here and now on this earth.

Are there no sideways or byways, Lord, where I can get peace and rest? Can I not call it a day and be rewarded with nice, fat ego satisfaction? Are there no dreams fit to soothe me into that lovely sleep of quiet? Are all those wishes so wrong, so childish? Then the Lord said, "Son, peace comes after the day's work when sweat and tears are mingled into a nectar too sweet to describe."

"Will I taste that sweetness, or will it be just for the greedy gods delighted by my agony and fatigue."

"Your fatigue, Erlo, is false. It is a result of not being willing to assume what is rightfully yours. Your complaint is paltry and even sinful, and totally blind to the needs of the millions upon millions waiting for a word of insight. They are waiting not for comfort or for peace, but for insight, which gives strength and energy. And through that insight comfort is provided to souls living in utter darkness who are seeking a spirit which is theirs and no one else's, seeking a Divine Essence, an eternal Being in their own make-up. You, who have experienced these insights and who have gone through so many revelations, must tell of your knowledge of lives past, and so reveal yourself."

Aquarius, are you there? What do you say? Or did you talk from within and was God's voice also your voice?

Hopelessly sad, I see Aquarius sitting head in hand on a small rock beside a road going through a meadow. It is a country road made of sand and stone. He smiles now that I am present, gets up and walks away, but then comes back and we stand face to face. "You are such a procrastinator, Erlo. I am waiting for the day – not too long from now – when I can be your daily companion. God's voice, my voice, your inner voice – where is the difference? Only your protesting Christian dogmatic voice is not mine. Daily, remember daily, you are a Light bearer too. I am young and my youth, as you see it, makes me moody And so I am sad, sad in you because the growth that is necessary for you to understand your task comes not in a moment, but is a daily building of psychic awareness for which you are eminently capable. So now on this short day, this dark day in which your writing helped to bring light and proportion to the universe, go out into the world of Christ's celebration. When you keep your alliance with me, your Self will lead you less sadly, more confidently, and an inner joy will replace the lament of a few pages before. But return to me tomorrow. Love, Aquarius. Awaiting your attention for our mutual growth."

December 23, 1967
New York City

Dark is the cloud hanging over me. It is darker than the moonless night, and I am listening to the gentle howling of the souls in despair. I hear them, but why answer? Didn't I climb up, no crawl up, from the underworld to find my bewildering way? Why help? Is there no god who helps, or devil, who pricks their bottoms and prods them on to this Hell, which is Earth? I hear them. But my ears want to shut them out. I can't see them, for they are down, down deep. Let God take care of them. He put them there.

Immediately, a voice responds: "Erlo, Erlo, slothful creature, God sends help through you. Through you he sends help. Do you hear the calls from the deep, Erlo? Descend and let the Blackness be your guide. Go down, down into the Darkness. The darker the night, the blacker the guide. Descend! Descend! Evil is thy song. Evil and wrong is the road of recovery. Evil, full of sting and pain – that is the way of descent into the Abyss where I live to redeem the unknown powers of the human psyche and mind. Go down, down, deeper down into the pestilence of stinking Death. There starts the Kundalini, there is the source of purest water distilled from the rot and decay of human unlived life. There, at that source, enter the Waters of Life and you, Erlo, are the descent, the descender and the plunger into the deep, foul mess to take part in the purity and purpose of all Hell on Earth. Your very name means the one from the underworld. Enter, Erlo! Enter the pool of Darkness and refresh your soul with the purest water of Hell, where Heaven starts and all life turns around in eternal bliss Then travel away, and not alone you will be. For then, contaminated with the pestilence of eternal bliss, you will go on your road of healing souls which you don't want to do, but which will happen just the same through you. Just be! Don't do!"

January 14, 1968
New York City

Bewilderment. Where goes my road? The old one is barred, and the map for the new one I do not have. How can we know where to go? It is baffling to me, who has always tried to go by landmarks and signs known to all of us. But now there is a Dark angel, who I don't know or see, blocking old roads and known ways.

I heard in the dark that a dear friend was King of France, one upon whom I had projected all. And John II of France was dark and evil. Still, he was named, the "Good." In a dream last night François Fénelon, my worldly host of my old castle, was tightening the gold knobs on a gold mandala plate while talking about the elegance of the Shahs of Persia. Rich foods were being served by servants who were not listening to what was said by their so-called "Mistress" or "Master." My anima was left out as she was not considered important, so I fed her from my plate, hoping the food would not be too rich for her. King Boris of Bulgaria, who was assassinated, cries out loud in my belly about the unbelievable atrocities done to him and to his suite.

All these goings on and here I sit in bewilderment – my most intimate attitude just worn out. As in my dream, I am not able even to drape around me the loincloth, which was made of the philosopher's stone. And we planned a picnic on the rock, which is the stone. And time after time I dream about the owners of the Fénelon château, which I love. Those dear people, putting their energies, their money and their lives into the continuation of that castle, which has been standing for over five hundred or six hundred years. Is that wrong? Is that right? Are worldly possessions important? Aren't they the dance for the golden calf?

I don't know any more. Am I not involved deeply enough in this world? Am I too much of the spirit and believe that all of the spirit becomes physical, or is there a law that only some of this world can become spiritual? Is it all the same? Has this world something to offer the spirit that it does not know? Spirit seeks quiet; earth seeks movement. There is an earth spirit I just don't know or comprehend.

"That is because, Erlo, you don't anchor in earth enough and stay connected with spirit too much," I hear Aquarius say. "The custodians of the physical world are the everlasting hosts for spirit and therefore the only house of redemption available to the human soul. Never have you seen the divine in the Dionysian. Away from flesh, you seek your salvation; in the Elysian fields you promise yourself total expression. But here on earth you pass up your opportunities and values. Earth, in all its evil, produces the gold, and the diamond – found so rough and crude – discovers its greatest expression through the cunning of the human crafts. If ever, ever you are to redeem the Black, the Unlived, the Dark, figure more and be wiser with the crude, rough possibilities of this earth.

"Why do you cringe and cramp your hands when you read about the surface mining despoiling the land? It is because of your love for nature and the land. The mining is not wrong, the method is. And so you are doing the same thing to yourself many, many times over – debasing your true nature with the civilized approach. The rape is to take place; it is experience, but the spoil is great. Never forget that the road leads downward for you into the Pit of Black Earth with all of its potential. John of France never ruined France! Boris could not save Bulgaria, nor his family. Thus the Black Light is as inscrutable as the Light of Christ. It seems they both weave their own patterns."

Yes! But I, Erlo, who by being human can bring awareness to God about himself, can also stay bewildered by these laws. Just as my being human is inherent in me, inherent also is my will to goodness and love as my only life goal. That is the way I am created. I, Erlo, am that part of my mandala spirit or Self which gathers unto itself the many sidedness of my existence, living not just as one personality but as several – now all dead, but one. I gather unto me all that was unlived in order to redeem myself and so, perhaps, the world, which is of less importance to me. I can't help but raise my voice in lament and horror at our complex human nature, and I leave this page with pain of existence and bewilderment of being.

January 16, 1968
New York City

Cold. Cold is the day. The sun has lost its warmth, and my inner heat is becoming dangerously overtaxed – so tells my dream. Clouds, miles thick, are between me and my life-giving force. Dense and grey, they bring their arctic weather for I am not willing to accept the consciousness of sunlight. I am not willing to listen to the words of my prophet. My ears are plugged, my eyes full of grey shadows. If I were not in danger from within, I would prefer the grey and the cold to the sun and the colors of life.

If ever I feared life, it is now. My instinctive being refuses to accept the spirit powers and shies away from their strength. Fear is in me, for those powers can push me to the brink of my sanity. Grey is my protection. Grey is my world of not knowing, not wanting to know what life holds in store for me. Today, I know there is a Light outside of me which I do not wish to reflect. Too bright is its glow; too powerful is its intent. That Light is too weird and too unknown for me to follow. Never, never would I, should I, or could I follow the Light of Aquarius if the danger from within me is not more fearful.

The Aquarian sun is coming up. Its dawn is now, and the thickest clouds cannot prevent that fact. I wish not to see the New Age. I'm too petrified to help the sun rise. I should know, though, that I can help with the sunrise of Aquarius, as I helped with the sunset of Pisces. The sign of the Fishes have had their way. Now, the proud Aquarius with his immensely rich, flowering, youthfulness is to come. And the thicker I make my grey clouds, the colder the atmosphere. I cannot heat my own house any more, for it is about to explode. Rather, I have to abolish the clouds of deliberate undoing and raise the temperature so that my house becomes warm from the coming sunshine. I cannot push down the inevitable rise of the dawn, nor can I ignore it. Aquarius is rising slowly, but his sun is ascending still too fast above the horizon to throw its light into my house and so warm my hearth and home. God have mercy, for with this rising power comes the Unlived Life of the race buried in the waters and carried by the Fishes. Now, all this potential is to become human. And I, fearful coward, am receiving, or better, becoming ready to receive his first direct ray.

The dawn is here. All over the world it is awaited and anticipated. Groups and individuals are being prepared for the first words, the translations of the Aquarian Light, and I prefer to stay numb. Greater sin could not be envisaged. I refuse being the first sacrificial lamb, the first son of God to receive in his warm, pulsating body the Light of Aquarius and carry it into consciousness.

April 28, 1968
Waverstead

It is as if I am far from glamour and power, and I quietly occupy myself with the small things in life. I feel, not for a moment, any inflation. Neither did I feel any last night. Rereading last night's writings, I feel stranger, stranger than fiction.

After dinner, Aquarius speaks: "Today was my first day on Earth in your body, Erlo. I felt like a newborn baby – unsteady, trusting, with a slight hold on life. Will life feed me? Will I survive? I have been nine years from the source of all life; I have come in nine years instead of nine months. Incredible. Unbelievable. But I came – hesitant, uncertain – with tears in my eyes and with sobriety. Now to start the second day. And then the third day, and so on into maturity, centuries from now.

"But I will never forget the first day at Waverstead, when I was in the numbed body of my first-born. The daffodils around the pond, the leaky dam, the grass coming up in tufts, the dandelions in full bloom; I see them now as I will in centuries to come. Through the eyes of Erlo, the bulb-grower's son, all is so strange, so different from before. I smell what you, Erlo, could not. Still numb from the birth, you are and will be, like me, curious and inquisitive. May the gods be with us. Jung and I were closer, but I was not on Earth yet. Always Christ pushed me aside until I established myself in Jung, but I was using the Jesus Christ body, not my own. Now the recalcitrant Erlo gave in. He is my first conquered kingdom. The rock, the prize of Peter, is now mine. The double Christ is standing on one rock; Carl-Erlo united on the stone, at last!

"Now, *avanti*! *Avanti*, into my glory – the aurora of my sun to shine forever unto the glory of God! God and I, Aquarius, are one – the sun's powers and energy to flow into my reign for thousands of years. My day has come. Humble and small, I enter the tired, exhausted psyche of my Erlo, who is hardly discernible from the tiniest speck of being. So small. So small the beginning. So great the moment. Thanks be to God for our smallness, a quality taught to me by Carl and Erlo, who are on one rock now – the stone called Peter. The two of them are as true priests – so small, and smaller still. Now, they are my messengers. Glory to them and to the Heavens; glory to a sense of wonder and to my Being, so unknown to me in Earth experiences. So be it. This was my day. A toast to the total unknown, countryman of Waverstead, and my eternal blessings and gratitude to your faithful wife."

May 11, 1968
Waverstead

When I accepted the spirit of Aquarius, I thought I was through dealing with that part of my life. However, that night I dreamt I came across the mummy of the Ram God, Aries, who was alive in his wrappings. He was being held prisoner by a guard and an anima figure and I was watching, while seated on an enormous bale of wheat straw, his struggles to free himself. The mummy was being transported on a train traveling from left to right and, in the dream, it was indicated that I had not passed my exams fully. Since I know a lot about the Ram God, I will tell you that he carries the soul of Osiris through the night, and he is also the one who carries out, in clay, the forming of the outer world. He molds the bodies of all of us, according to the spirit of Darkness. He is a form of Lucifer. I don't think I have ever been so afraid of a spirit, even when I recall encountering the spirit of Daytime and Light. Apparently uncharted roads, unknown fields and worlds are to be brought into consciousness.

Where to begin? And if I don't begin, there is nothing but nightmarish horror. As shown in my dream, a total debacle for the living world will ensue. What can I do? I have to deal with the world of the shadow, and the Ram God carries the sun at night, brings the wheat of Osiris to the underworld, and gives the black bread to those who have no eyes to see anywhere. To them the Ram God, Amon, is their god, and Aquarius knows this and can live it. He can live the seen and the unseen, the manifest and the unmanifest. That makes me the Redeemer of the underworld as well.

Lord, what to do next! I am so horrified, so dreadfully numb from horror. Where is life? I stand beyond feeling pain, beyond feeling terror. Nothingness. All is within me, for the King of the Night is to enter this world. Osiris of the Night is to be reborn. The terror of power – God's own power – has made me hopelessly numb. That power preferred the fish to man. As fish we swam, and now the man of the Night is to return. Light and Darkness are encased in me, Erlo. Terror is around and life is not. There is no eternity. There is no endless performance of man. Death takes over in darkness, and Nothing is, and in that ignorance the people lived not knowing of eternity, and thus the Ram God, Aries, spoke.

"I don't tear my hair. I don't rave and run around, because numbness is the mummy's role. I don't talk. I don't act and I don't see. But I hear and I can listen. But I am dead. Dead. And no Light is in Darkness; all instinct belonging to that connection is dead. There is nothing but death. And death has no Light, only putrefaction. So, I am now dead in a live body, and there is no Light to help me out, no instinctive awakening. Death is death is death. No cycle can change it. The world does not go around on its axis. There is nothing but death. Although the sun shines, nothing happens because the night is not important and cannot fertilize the day. The Earth dries up and is brown, and the night stultifies and is grey.

"And so that psyche exists. There is where I live. There is where I am now. What next? For in this place there is no resurrection. No Easter. No fertility. And unless Erlo changes, this barrenness will be the state of the world, and his world. The moon and sun will disappear, and only Erlo will be – if he can be – the bearer of the eternal change, the bearer of all that is human, the carrier of the Darkness of the flesh with the eternal Light of the sun.

"But Erlo's flesh is numb. He is seated on the wheat straw and thinks it is not edible. He thinks only grain is, but the rest is chaff to him. For what is the flesh of that old horror, the Christ? What does he know about the darkness of the body, or of the sun? His glory is in the heavens; barren, barren heavens from which he pisses. But where are his senses? Where is the enlivening love of the New Light. It was pissed away from his pinnacle of the Cross, his Golgotha. The penis without balls, where is that barrenness to lead to?

"To hell with him. To hell with the one-sided Light of an Osiris. Blind! Blind at night is that Light unless it is carried in my body, unless I give humanity the carrier of their soul. For only I, through my body, can carry that New Light of Darkness into the night and down into the steep Abyss. Nothing! Nothing there is, unless at night I, the Ram God, I, Aquarius, I, Erlo, carry that Darkness of Light and that Light of Darkness. Who dares to raise to the cross the human body, resurrect it and deny the body? (Oh God, why did'st thou forsake me?) Only Almighty God, with infinite cruelty, dares to achieve a creation so horrendous and magnificent and so totally inexplicable.

"That same God who took, gives now again. Unbearable is that pain of becoming again the Night Traveler with the glowing, penetrating Light; a Light so cool, so all pervading that even secrets shed their lights and reveal a truth equal to the Almighty power of the One and Only. God is now again in full descent to the glory of being human. No more the cold-bloodedness of the last God of Light, of Daytime; here now again I am, unwinding my wrappings, one after one, to be human all the way. No more the way of the Lamb, but rather the maturity of the Ram with all I represent.

"Oh God, have mercy on humanity, for I am stalking ferociously where I cannot graze peacefully. Here I come again, Night-Brother to Daytime-Sister; the return of the Messianic of the flesh of the night – full-blooded – reclaiming the mummified psyches to be adored and venerated, for within me is the Light, the soul of the Ram God. In the darkest hour, my Light shines to bring forth wisdom and awareness. Lord, have mercy on my first son, Aquarius. He and I are one. Humanity does not know what it can see of the death side of life. Humanity gropes in darkness and sees nothing, but with the help of my Sister-Daytime I establish a glow and a penetration which will make no eye blink, just widen with wonder and horror of this Earth creation. Then the Christ will be warm and walk on this Earth in a body of flesh and bones. All, all will be One. Such is the power of Aquarius and his first-born son, Erlo.

"Now on your way, my son, to Aquarius' fulfillment. Step into my powers, which are Aquarius'. Not even he, Aquarius, knows this, for unto him is born a complete mensch in whom the flesh and soul have equal say, in whom the Light is never extinguished. Cain and Abel will be united and married to their sisters, Shadow and Death. The Light will not go out where Aquarius rules, for the Black Diamond in the back of his head will shineth forever more."

June 16, 1968
Zürich

Slowly, oh so slowly I, Aquarius, am returning from my sojourn through the unconscious of Erlo and the deeper layers of Darkness below the threshold of consciousness which have not been touched upon for aeons, if ever. Never shall I try to be quick and harsh again, for what I have beheld on my travels through these regions of Darkness is fit only for gods to look at. No human eye could stand looking into this Deep Darkness, this Pit of Despair and Non-Being which has now been aroused through my descent unto Earth. My youth is gone, my energies are exhausted and I have not even started my reign.

I did not know, I did not know, oh Lord. I did not know about your creation. Have mercy on me, the ruling God to be! Have mercy on my youth, for already grey is my hair. Seated and settled on the back of the Ram God I traveled where only beasts and gods could go, but this time I had the awareness of Erlo. I could judge with his consciousness. And his fatigue this morning is the burden I, Aquarius, put on him in order to come back into my own.

But my own can never again be as it was before, for unto me was shown the nether world through the eyes of the Ram. I know that I knew of the Christ. I know that I knew of the antichrist, the Black Brother, but how, how ever was I to know about the deeper regions of Darkness if not another god had pleaded to me and said: "God to come and ruler, ruler of the aeon now at its beginning, come and see what happened and did not happen in my reign."

So Aries, the Ram, spoke unto me and with human fears in his heart and head, he said: "Oh great ruler of the New Divine plan, let me come to your help and teach what I didn't know when I uttered my last words on the cross; 'Oh God, why hast thou forsaken me?' Then I, the Ram, went through a Hell which was different from ever before. For in Christ's era I was excluded from all awareness and so, from afar, I looked upon the stage of life, which was so totally different from my own world. I saw the building of empires. I saw the structures erected to send rockets to the moon and to Venus. I saw the scratch made on Mars, and its orbit invaded by man-made machines, extensions of the human consciousness reaching far into the cosmos. And then and there I saw the deepening Darkness of a forgotten life. The further human consciousness reached, the deeper the Darkness. And so I rested. But deep, deep down, my tears were flowing slowly through men's unconscious, and where there were no tears there were icicles, so sharp, so deep in their penetration that murder and devastation and barrenness on Earth and in the human psyche were the result.

"How ever was I, the Ram, to come back to my beloved world? Was I forever to be on the cross of the Nile? Was my road forever to be called the Devil's route? So I lay down, as my feet could not hold me, and deeper and deeper was my sleep. Then, oh noble Aquarius, came my dream. It was a dream of resurrection whereby I again would return, not as before, but in a greater measure than ever. My Ram's eye beheld a vision of my place in a cavalcade of gods and rulers. Proudly I would walk in stately fashion, becoming to my own dignity, right behind a resurrected Christ living in you, my beloved Aquarius and Erlo. I would again be alive, this time following and listening and learning more than ever. Know for all time, my noble Aquarius, in you we gods unite with greater possibility of consciousness than before. So that you will know more about your reign, I requested you to mount my back and ride the circuit of the Zodiac, as I know the way through the Darkness of Light and can show you the course of the ten unknown regions. Your court, and Christ's court, I will not enter unless you, Aquarius, ask for them to be shown unto you through my eyes."

Oh my dear Erlo, beloved son of mine, I went on that journey and then I asked the Ram to be gracious enough to show me the court of the Piscean Age, Christ's domain and, if possible, the vista of what is to come in mine. The proud Aries, who had been so steadfast in the darkest Abyss or on the highest regions of the Zodiacal courts, almost lost balance as his legs buckled, unable to carry my weight on his back through the Christian era. Feelings became numb in me as they are now in you. I didn't know, as I dismounted, what to do until I took the lead and led my guide. I took my beloved Ram by his horns fist, then folded my arms around his neck to lead him gently through the Christian era. Many times he stopped from exhaustion, but I knew if I would leave him behind my reign would fail, for I cannot deny any god. I must accept all that is. If I will comprehend everything is a different matter; that depends on humanity's capacity for consciousness. But I, as a god and your ruler, I knew that I must be all or nothing which, my dearly beloved son, you have taught me already. The Ram Aries, that Divine See-er of Darkness, that beloved friend and predecessor of mine, has shown me the world of Zodiacal monsters through his eyes and I am a wiser god today.

I, Aquarius, will write more about my journey tomorrow, for both you, Erlo, and I are too exhausted for the moment to continue. Send your blessings and love to the Ram God, who loves you dearly, for his Light came again into being through your consciousness. His Redeemer he calls you, while Christ was his divine killer-priest by whom he was taught forgiveness also, forgiveness so that he could accept the drama of life on a universal scale. So be it for today.

Just now, in the bathroom, Aquarius said unto me: "Oh Erlo, oh Erlo, where do we go from here? Will I ever succeed in what I want now to accomplish? I always thought I just had to rule. Oh, my God! Help me! Have mercy! Oh, no, no! I have a goal. I have a purpose. No, please, no. But I have a wish. Lord, grant me consciousness and awareness, greater even than possessed by the divine Carl Gustav. As he was among men, so I want to be among gods."

June 17, 1968
Zürich

I would like to write in this book today but I cannot listen to my friend, Aquarius. I will work on my dreams, instead.

I was deeply touched by the fact that Aquarius wished for greater consciousness. His rule might, indeed, then bring greater glory to humanity and so to God. How heavy will be his task and what chaos there will be unless we can also hold on to the Light of Christ, hold on to our morals and our sensitivities as we travel through this dense psyche called Earth – the greatest of chemical vessels there ever was or is in our Solar System. What opportunity!

June 18, 1968
Zürich

"Hey, Erlo, where are you? In order to finish this diary you will have to be daily at my side, for I'm pressing you for time. Each time I speak to you, I speak to thousands, if not millions! Each time, I see things clearer through your eyes; humanity, then, can see clearer through mine. There is a time element involved, as this writing has to become known before too many crises crowd in on the consciousness of mankind.

"Don't you hear people fighting and shouting in the streets and in the corridors of the temples of learning? The spirit of Christ is diminishing and mine is not known. The multitude do not know how many times they have to turn corridors that lead into blind alleys of the mind. Don't you hear what they are crying for? In all those wild hordes you hear the rumble of my spirit, but no trumpet call has come forth to tell them about the holiness of their own individual being. Not for nothing did I ride the Ram. Neither did I cross the course of the Zodiacal signs in order to stay rambunctious or adventurous with the souls of men. I have learned fast in the last few years through the eyes and ears of many Jungian followers, led by an unknown few. Now, I have to tell those uproarious youngsters and men of the future that their human dignity should dictate the next chapter of their enterprises. My power, my spirit, which was so denied by stodgy minds, so feared by conscious intellect, will penetrate everyone without fail – either to be welcomed or to be shunned.

"Tomorrow, after breakfast, sit down and receive my message faithfully, for it will be my code of the future. Fear not, just write what comes up, as you did tonight."

June 19, 1968
Zürich

When the thunder is over the lake at Zürich, the gods are near. Pain and fatigue are good teachers but bad companions, one might say. In each and all of us there is a cosmos, a microcosm equal to the macrocosm. But who wants to know; worse still, who is able to know or register the voices within, since each of us has our own hierarchy. I refuse. I rebel. Aquarius, I don't want to preach, and unless you come forth with a powerful thing that sweeps me off my feet, I won't write.

"I know, Erlo, we had better quit. It is not the time yet. You are not ground down finely enough to take my message today. There was too much mental stimulation. You analyzed and attended colloquiums at the Jung Institute, and the spirit, my spirit, is out of reach tonight."

July 11, 1968
Bad Ragaz

It is thundering in the Valley of the Dead. The bells are tolling everywhere. Aquarius is doleful, deeply disturbed; he is calling on God, on Erlo, to be the sacrificial lamb again. Isha Jahu lies on his bier, his guts out, his legs loose from his body; for centuries, for aeons, timeless agony has cursed his being. Wasn't he a prophet? Wasn't he the Prince of Prophets? And there he lies – still now – disemboweled like a Judas, separated by the hand of God as executed by the hands of a jealous stink of a king. Will there ever be a union of Heaven and Earth? Will there be, forever, a schism between the Heavenly voices and the Earthly realities? Will God never know that All is One? Has he ever any idea of marriage? Doesn't he want to embrace Earth as it is, counterpart and twin of his own Being? Christ asked for his Judas, and then his wholeness came about in

Aquarius, but I, Erlo, am still separated. In me lives the agony of the torn prophet.

Isaiah was full of love for earth and for life. He lived spirit unhampered and so was deep in his body, he thought – not knowing the powers of earth. He strode forth in divine wrath against all that was not good and right and beloved in the eyes of the Lord, his Lord he thought, who was of Moses, and Yahweh, and David and Saul. His was the voice of righteousness which thundered through the ages, as it is thundering now in this Rhine Valley.

But there is another voice now which I hear – the voice of the motor car and of the truck, which is right under my window. It is an earth voice of the twentieth century, hideous, and yet so beneficial at times. I have learned, Lord, I, Isha Jahu, your servant, I have learned much, but not enough. Not enough yet. For deep within me, from far away, far away from beyond space and time, there cries now a voice awakened by Aquarius, the new god. His sun will now protect what neither Aries nor Pisces could allow to live. Do you hear, Lord? No. Well, listen, you dumb force of the Eternal Now. Listen! And so will I, seated here at my window in Ragaz, bathed in tears never shed before.

Do you remember my descent to this earth? Do you know that moment when Jung gave the call for the next aeon to be heralded, and, Emmanuel, the son of a maiden, would announce a new era? As in my vision beyond space, which mirrored itself on this earth,[1] you, you Lord, called for help and I answered. I descended to take on this dense psyche of yours, to take on this manifestation called earth. All of me came without holding back an atom of my vibrant Being, only to be sawed and torn apart in the end as the price of my glory of Being. Yes, I took it, I did. I did not fail you, oh Lord. I came back. You saw me as Alfrenennon, as Peter, and as Paul. You saw me fight as Coeur de Leon and Gottfried of Bouillon. I did not withdraw from the spirit of the gory affairs of war and

[1] As Isaiah's vision of God on his throne asking for help.

greed. I took it. I lived and relived, time after time. Too many times to mention did I take your thunder and your lightning, which is just now shaking this château and undoing the electricity. But you did not shake my trust in you. Our covenant withstood the ages. However, far, far off in regions yet untouched by civilization there was a part of me, a part of my true Self, that was withdrawn on account of the pain and the tearing of tissues – for the world was not ready to receive it. Alone, alone I was. Part of my soul lay beyond the reach of any earth or flesh, dead to the incarnating round of spirit.

So I lived in my tower dungeon until Aquarius' call came when making the rounds through the courts of the Zodiac, enlivening not just the unlived but touching, with a tender hand, the wounds of the past. My life blood, seeping away so slowly, now was touched by the divine Aquarius seated on the Ram, who could not protect me and was sadly looking away. Blood and tears re-established a sense of awareness in me and then he, Aquarius, prayed for my total restoration, prayed for a vigorous return to Earth of all of me – now existing in Erlo.

But the pain of my Isaian death had to be experienced emotionally. Without that ritual, no return was possible. How many times haven't I looked, after awakening myself from my stupor, through the trellis of my self-protecting dungeon to see that the opportunity was not there? Floods of blood of the sacrifice passed my windows and touched my foundation. From that blood arose psalms and curses alike – strange music of the unlived – rhythms of the agony.

Now I am planning my return through rivers of agony of my own. My strength will be restored. Again, I will live side by side with a physical manifestation and be aware of endless difficulties. I will slowly creep back into life. Lord, have mercy. From far beyond time, I come. My descent touches the unloved and the despised. Aquarius, don't fail those you aroused, for a second time of such separation of my soul and my eternal Being might make me lose consciousness forever.

There is no illusion in me. The road will be hard and the going heavy. But if I can maintain myself and Aquarius' love is with me, and I love and am true to my way of awareness, then something very different and profound can happen. I will touch earth with other feet, and from deep within this earth a force called upon will arise which might give different and new powers to the plough and the sword. The sickle will disappear, and the hammer will build a new empire. Strange as it may seem, I will live in anticipation of Aquarius' revelations. I have seen his smile and his Christ-like warmth, and love broke my dungeon. The thunder is over and the electricity went on the moment I wrote: "Christ-like warmth and love." Synchronicity will bring about the wonders when the feet of unlived life touch this earth again.

The birds are singing once more, and the clouds slowly mount the Alps in view of my window. The earth is refreshed, and far, far away I hear the rumbling voices of the thunder spreading the news that Isha-Erlo has his ancient new feet again. So, I sit quietly in anticipation of the changes to come. The Book of Changes. Our life. May my earthly body receive the full blessings of this hour.

I just read this day's writing to my darling Ann. It is twelve noon, and the bell in the church tower here in Ragaz is ringing happily. Two thousand seven hundred years were spanned – and now a second church bell joins the first.

July 14, 1968
Bad Ragaz

It is the quiet before dawn. The earth cools off, and for a moment it is colder than the night. It is the moment of suspense and anticipation, and fear creeps into the house of the father. The negatives arrive. Brainy and dehumanized ideas arise. Will it truly happen? Will I be taken out of the gutter of the street into my father's mansion? Will all come about as I wrote? Or, am I mistaken?

The moment of doubt is the moment before the revelation. The house of my mother is too tired to celebrate, although I arranged the flowers of spring for mother's birthday. But I do it hastily and not with care, for the affirmation of the *coniunctio* has not happened. Although I know all will be right, and all is arranged, this is the moment of doubt – a moment as holy and as necessary, as always. For without this doubt, no faith is built, and by doubting we can come to awareness.

There is no inflation in me. Aquarius seems far away, meditating his first steps with the united Erlo, who is healed but still convalescing; tired all through his body and fearful because he is human and knows about failure and pain. Is Aquarius fearful? What is he contemplating? Is he wondering what the feet of the unlived will bring forth?

There is no thunder in the sky. The haze is around the mountains, and calmness prevails. *Über allen Gipfeln gibt es "Ruhe."* It is a state of wonder. The unknown next step is contemplated. But what can happen in a body so fatigued? Rest. It is Sunday. Be of good mood and walk in the woods with your Ann. But should I? My first dream in Ragaz was a week ago. In it, a voice said, "The wind blows over the waters. Time for action." Now, I will rest on this Bastille Day.

The Song of the Bardo Lady in White

Green, green is my land and never, never any more will I return to the land of the living. Neither will the land of the dead be able to touch me or to conquer my spirit, for here in my green silence do I want to do penance for my sins and the pestilence I spread on Earth by my mistaken spirituality. I hobble along on my feet, half rotten from unexpressed agonies forced upon me by a curse so cruel that mentioning it would wither normal men to shivering, shaking corpses with numb souls looking through the windows of their eyes on the scourged Earth.

For two thousand years have I shuffled along the green world of silence, neither alive nor dead. If I had died, I might have been reborn and so not know any more the curse of the aeon. Had I stayed alive on Earth, I would have become a shaking corpse of a soul. But here in the Bardo, in the silence of the green, I walk and walk, shuffling along my path, not seeing, not wanting to know the curse fully, evading clarity, inviting numbness with only one will, one wish, one purpose – stay here, in the green. Don't walk away from this land of potential. Don't enter the rounds of mortality, for nothing, nothing is accomplished. Christianity would amputate my feet. Nobleness would kill my purpose. And the snakes of merciful prayers would try to endear themselves to me in order to coil around my heart and sting my soul into the oblivion of Christian charity, thereby undoing my life and purposeful pursuit for a truth in which good or evil could be evaluated as they are – tools of my divinity. In themselves, these tools are nothing but means to an end – meaningless, unless pitched into the battle to extract the Light of consciousness.

So I shuffled, my left foot more wounded and painful than my right. My right leg is better, because encounters with the knowledge of the good came my way each time an immortal soul passed through the green world into the Light to start its inevitable return to mortal life. But where is the knowledge which can cure my left foot? Cursed be to man-created God, denuding him of his left hand. Cursed be the blackness in man's mind that undoes the purpose of the Darkness, and damn the evil that undoes Evil as carrier of its own divine Light. So dark are the stairs, darker than the Pit of Hell, on which my thoughts have to travel up and up into the bestial beast called Man. Awake! Awake! Call me back to life and immortal mortality! End my wandering in my green world! "Come to my help!" I cried, to all who passed through.

But I was just a fool, a hag, a bastard-witch. So I went on and on in circles, but never in spirals. In circles I kept myself alive and breathed pestilence in order to maintain myself on the path.

Now, comes the day. The gatekeeper, delighting in my agony with his black, smirking smile, had at last his prey. He said he could relieve me of my curse if he would succeed in trapping a soul, ready by destiny, to accept the cruelty of seeing his Christian anima grilled the way he was grilled once for the sake of Christianity. This soul he could lure to the gatekeeper's house on his path through the green meadow. I said, "Go ahead, you bastard; no one yet has the power of insight to bring me back to the living." So it was. He came through the ever-open gate and halted. At first, I only saw his Light. It was blue and iridescent, a strange numinous Light. And then I saw him – the Star of the Eclipse of Moon and Sun. Behold! There he stood! And suddenly, he turned around and went back through the gate to his mortal habitat.

Now I know my time has come, and I will return to Earth after many aeons to fulfill a life and a destiny, foreign to mankind as yet, that will entail the Darkness as a source of consciousness. Back will be the day of human counterbalance. The snake will curl around the Cross, and from the blackness of my eternal rounds of green silence will emerge the fruits of my meditations – all for the benefit of Dark imminence carrying with it a precious gift of consciousness to this parched world.

I will unlock the wells and springs and bathe my feet in their healing waters. For unto me was shown a Light for mankind to follow and to lift the curse of Christian impunities. Now, indeed, the Lord Christ can get into his own and enjoy the Light-giving Darkness of his Brother-Twin. The day of revelation is at hand, and soon I will walk the meadows of sunshine and the lanes of night to reappear each morning in the wisdom of people's dreams. Thanks to my scribe, carrying the Blue Light of Darkness, for not withdrawing his love from the gatekeeper while he was grilling cruelly the lifeless bodies, the remnants of Christian moralities as made by an age-old dogma. Praise and thanks to the Lord. And to Erlo.

July 22, 1968
Bad Ragaz

The Aquarian Way

What is this personal road called "The Aquarian Way?" It is high noon, and slowly the bell intones twelve majestic gong-like strikes as I sit here at my beautiful window in the Hotel Schloss Ragaz. The mountain tops are powdered white with the snow fallen a few days ago. The sun shines now and the weather is like spring. Cool. Crisp. And delightful. But it is summer, and the first roses are long since gone. All signs of spring have matured into the fullness of summer. The leaves are developed. The fruit is ripening, and the fall will come by late September, in two months.

There is where I come in. The multicolored fall is my season, before the winter comes with the eternal everlasting aspects of nature awaiting patiently, through snow and sleet, the rains of spring. The flower seeds, full of the intense beauty of their later growth, stay in the dark earth, asleep, not aware. That form of life for the human is now to change. The avant-garde of the Aquarian human will be like trees; some will denude, others will stay green.

But in my short season, have I shown all my colors? Have I been the sum total of all I can be and am destined to be? Or, have I been a result of a father and a mother neurosis; an intelligent, struggling individual with integrity and sobriety, some erudition, and many failings. Since I have worked for thirty-four years on becoming what I really am, what do I know about myself? My psychic ancestors have had their say and their shadows have been cleansed as far as I was able to do it. And now with Aquarius pressing at the door, and knocking and knocking and demanding with his archaic power, I have come to the conclusion that unless I'm very much, very much myself, my unique Erlo, Erlo-self, I would fail the very thing in which Aquarius is most interested: the individual.

My God, having gone so far, what am I? Where am I? What questions to ask now? Am I just a scribe for a god, a new tool useful for a couple of years then to be interred like a seasonal flower seed? What on earth is this uniqueness about?

This morning I had a terrible, disgusting dream letting me know that the toilet paper I use is about the most personal thing I have right now. Well, it is something with which to start. It makes me think of the lotus, a flower with its roots in the slime, or the scarab, a divine creature which lays its eggs in the dung. And so, perhaps, in this symbol is a profound root. Frankly, at this moment the divine process does not interest me a whole lot. I am right now very much in search of a personal approach towards this manifestation called Erlo. From my writings I know about multiplicity, the many-sided aspects of each and every one of us. But in all this profusion, where the hell am I? Yes, I accept the toilet paper, but that is not all. If I would identify with that symbol I could call myself a heap of a four-letter word. Although the Chinese refer to that word as the flower of the body, I don't. Neither am I interested in the perfection of the lotus, nor in the dull shape, endlessly repeated, of the scarab. I won't buy that analogy. I refuse that sameness.

Now I hear roars of laughter from Aquarius. "So, you try now to find out who you are?" He is terribly amused and slaps his thigh. "You dumbbell, you eternal fool! Don't you know that you are not a one of anything, but a multiple design with life's secret in the middle of it?"

"Like a mandala? I hate that! I don't want to be a multiple design."

"Listen, Mr. Erlo, schlemiel, you are that whether you like it or not. All of your writing points to it. All you can have – and you know it already – is a very personal approach to your own life and design. Your personal reaction is the goal; your own awareness is your only value. Therein lies your uniqueness. Go after that which pleases you; admire that which is admirable in your own eyes. You are from the West and so you identify with spirit, and through that identification enter your life on spiritual principles. In your deepest unconscious you are also from the East, and therefore identification with the earth plays its role.

"In this overall pattern I am showing you now, in this design, you have to react as Erlo van Waveren, born in Hillegom, Holland, son of a merchant father and a mother who was the daughter of a marine insurance expert. Through your life design you developed, and in its maze of influences you would lose your way if there was not inborn in your personality a precious jewel, my Aquarian jewel – the individual choice – and it is wholly yours. Reactions belong to your personality. You can't escape them. When you are aware of your own and not in the grip of some ancestral neurosis, you are already further along on the path. But the path is the ancestral neurosis. It is ancient and full of entanglement of life's forces, never to be undone, really – always there. However, when you see the design and where you are in it, you can form your opinion and with my jewel – the personal choice – work like a god. There it is! You design, unknown to the Godhead, the most precious of all stage plays. It is watched at in deepest reverence for, on a minute scale, you form a world of your own; you form the essence of your diamond. There is no word precious enough to mention its value.

"Now, remember the dream-vision in which the World-Spirit came to you through the 'breathing hole of eternity' and sat himself at the end of your bed, asking you to seat yourself in his lap in order to spray your semen in the design of a peacock's tail on his chest. This act is requested from you and everyone on this earth. The Lord Maitreya, the Buddha to come, needs and wants this most intimate contact from you. He wants your potential, not in the form of ego wishes alone, not in the form of your personality alone, but in the total form of the life of the Eternal Return – your immortality expressed in the life of your seed. That life is short-lived on this earth, but immensely powerful and the essence of all our human survival. So, in this multiple design of personal and impersonal, seat yourself in the lap of this Buddha in order that his consciousness will be affected for the ages to come.

"Nothing is lost of your life, as you know from your writing. Construct this life of your own; build it with mortar and stone, both earth-like products. It can be made by you as mortar, and shaped by you into stone. Although the astrologers since time immemorial have spoken about your fate, that design is already known by the muses and the gods. What we, however, do not know, and are in constant wonder about is how you, as part of humanity, use our gifts and create the world unknown to us. You are the one who creates the psychic atmosphere. Your consciousness and awareness, the Divine essence of your life experience, is what we watch as gods in amazement, awe, and horror alike.

"It is up to you, Erlo, to create out of your own life experience a life which is true to what you are now at this time; a life true to your coloring, your awareness, your leanings, loves, likes, dislikes and hatreds. In your precious suffering of all we gods give lies that complicated thing called uniqueness, that pin-point made of a cosmic design now named Erlo. Erlo, an individual on his own, unprotected but for his own laws – the laws of survival, not just of earth-life but of eternal-life as well. God in your own right among the gods of God's right.

"Form your own opinion. Live your own color and design. Create your world, and through its creation, measure the greater design of those aspects far outreaching you. Be aware of your own Divine essence in your lopsided personal manifestation, which is different from all others and on account of that difference is most important and all-important in the eyes of the Lord. What, oh what disaster, if your off-balanced way of experiencing life was left behind and you would become one with the masses. All music would stop and in utter despair God would pluck you away from this earth as a useless experiment. Loss of soul is a frightful dilemma; the personality not able to carry spirit is loss of soul.

"So, peculiar, crazy, sweet Erlo, with a long line of sins and troubles and pleasures, live day to day. Build every moment true to yourself and I, the Aquarian, will breathe deeply and say: 'Thank God! There walks another one of my sons. God's son on Earth. Blessed be his name.'"

ENGLISH PUBLICATIONS BY **DAIMON**

Susan Bach – *Life Paints its Own Span*
E.A. Bennet – *Meetings with Jung*
George Czuczka – *Imprints of the Future*
Heinrich Karl Fierz – *Jungian Psychiatry*
von Franz / Frey-Rohn / Jaffé – *What is Death?*
Liliane Frey-Rohn – *Friedrich Nietzsche*
Yael Haft – *Hands: Archetypal Chirology*
Siegmund Hurwitz – *Lilith, the first Eve*
Aniela Jaffé – *The Myth of Meaning*
– *Was C.G. Jung a Mystic?*
– *From the Life und Work of C.G. Jung*
– *Death Dreams and Ghosts*
Verena Kast – *A Time to Mourn*
– *Sisyphus*
Hayao Kawai – *Dreams, Myths and Fairy Tales in Japan*
James Kirsch – *The Reluctant Prophet*
Mary Lynn Kittelson – *Sounding the Soul*
Rivkah Schärf Kluger– *The Gilgamesh Epic*
Paul Kugler – *Jungian Perspectives on Clinical Supervision*
Rafael López-Pedraza– *Hermes and his Children*
– Cultural Anxiety
Alan McGlashan – *The Savage and Beautiful Country*
– Gravity and Levity
Gitta Mallasz (Transcription) – *Talking with Angels*
C.A. Meier – *Healing Dream and Ritual*
– *A Testament to the Wilderness*
Laurens van der Post – *The Rock Rabbit and the Rainbow*
R.M. Rilke – *Duino Elegies*
Miguel Serrano – *C.G. Jung and Hermann Hesse, A Record of Two Friendships*
Susan Tiberghien – *Looking for Gold*
Ann Ulanov – *The Wizards' Gate*
Ann & Barry Ulanov – *Cinderella and Her Sisters: The Envied and the Envying*

Jungian Congress Papers:

Jerusalem 1983 – *Symbolic and Clinical Approaches*
Berlin 1986 – *Archetype of Shadow in a Split World*
Paris 1989 – *Dynamics in Relationship*
Chicago 1992 – *The Transcendent Function*
Zürich 1995 – *Open Questions in Analytical Psychology*

Available from your bookstore or from our distributors:

In the United States:

Continuum
P.O. Box 7017
La Vergne, TN 37086
Phone: 800-937 5557
Fax: 615-793 3915

Chiron Publications
400 Linden Avenue
Wilmette, IL 60091
Phone: 800-397 8109
Fax: 847-256 2202

In Great Britain:

Airlift Book Company
8 The Arena
Enfield, Middlesex EN3 7NJ
Phone: (0181) 804 0400
Fax: (0181) 804 0044

Worldwide:

Daimon Verlag Hauptstrasse 85 CH-8840 Einsiedeln Switzerland
Phone: (41)(55) 412 2266 Fax: (41)(55) 412 2231
e-mail: Daimon@compuserve.com Write for our complete catalog!